Cambridge El P9-EDU-939

THE
APOLOGY OF SOCRATES

PLATO

THE APOLOGY OF SOCRATES

✳✳✳✳✳✳✳✳✳✳✳✳✳✳✳✳✳✳✳✳✳✳✳✳✳✳✳✳✳✳✳✳

EDITED BY
ADELA MARION ADAM

CAMBRIDGE UNIVERSITY PRESS

CAMBRIDGE
LONDON · NEW YORK · MELBOURNE

Published by the Syndics of the Cambridge University Press
The Pitt Building, Trumpington Street, Cambridge CB2 1RP
Bentley House, 200 Euston Road, London NW1 2DB
32 East 57th Street, New York, NY 10022, USA
296 Beaconsfield Parade, Middle Park, Melbourne 3206, Australia

ISBN 0 521 05958 5

First published 1914
Reprinted 1925 1930 1937
1949 1951 1959 1964
Reset 1969
Reprinted 1972 1974 1976 1977

Printed in Great Britain at the
University Press, Cambridge

PREFACE

This edition, which is intended for those who have only lately begun the study of Greek, is based on the edition by my husband in the Pitt Press series. Where no simplification or abridgement seemed necessary, I have not hesitated to use the original wording, but the notes have been for the most part, and the introduction entirely, rewritten. A vocabulary has also been added. I have made considerable use of Mr H. Williamson's edition, published since my husband's lifetime. I am very glad that Professor Burnet's most interesting work, *Greek Philosophy*, *Thales to Plato*, appeared just in time to enable me to consult it when writing the introduction.

A. M. A.

Cambridge
3 August 1914

CONTENTS

INTRODUCTION

The life of Socrates, like that of most thinkers whose work has left a permanent mark upon the world, was singularly devoid of external events. He was born at Athens in the year 469 B.C. His father was a sculptor. His education seems to have been of the ordinary type in vogue at that day, consisting of music (including grammar and literature) and gymnastics. In later life he showed that he had a considerable acquaintance with contemporary science, but he probably acquired this familiarity for himself, without the aid of regular instruction.

A doubtful tradition says that he started life as a sculptor. If he ever began a craft, he did not carry it on for long, but soon made it the main business of his life to hold conversations, indoors and outdoors, summer and winter, always in a shabby old garment and barefooted ('to flout the shoemakers' as a comic writer says), with any man, slave or citizen, obscure or a member of the highest Athenian society, whom he could induce to listen to him. Though he did not shirk the military service that fell to his share, he never went out of Athens on his own account, and was laughed at by his friends for needing to be shown round places near the town, as if he were a stranger engaged in sight-seeing.

In the *Apology*, 20E ff., we read that the oracle at Delphi replied to an enthusiastic admirer of Socrates that no wiser man existed. The date of this pronouncement is unknown, but Socrates must have been already an outstanding personality at Athens, or his friend would not have put the question to the oracle. According to the *Apology*, Socrates, astonished at the answer, directed all his energy to a search for the reason why wisdom should be attributed to him, when he himself was conscious that he was not in the least wise. He therefore set to work to question persons in various classes of society, who might presumably possess some wisdom. He found that they, while far from wise, were ignorant of their lack of wisdom; and he concluded that he was wiser than the rest of the world to this extent, that he was aware of his ignorance.

His investigations convinced him that there was something very much amiss with his country, and that the first step in the path of reform was to bring home to his fellow-citizens their false conceit of knowledge, and to implant in them a longing for truer wisdom. To this object he applied himself unceasingly, so that he neglected all ordinary means of earning a livelihood, or acquiring a position of importance in the city, and naturally his unsparing criticism of persons who stood high in their own estimation and in that of their contemporaries brought him many enemies. His zeal for knowledge also, and disregard of conventionalities made him an excellent mark for the shafts of comic playwrights. We possess several fragments making mock of his poverty and love of talk; but by far the most important of these attacks is the play of Aristophanes entitled the *Clouds*, produced in 423 B.C., when Socrates was aged 46. In the *Clouds* Socrates and his disciples are represented as physically degenerate, heretical or atheistical in their religious opinions, wasting their intellectual powers on scientific trifles, and masters of unscrupulous argument.

Against these onslaughts we must set the pictures of Socrates drawn for us by Plato and Xenophon, both of them his friends and disciples. Here we are confronted by a great difficulty. On the one hand, in all moral and personal characteristics, the original of both portraits is manifestly the same; on the other, the Socrates of Plato's greater works exhibits a power of thought far more profound and comprehensive than anything to be found in Xenophon. Some scholars have lately gone so far as to say that Xenophon knew little about Socrates, and was incapable of understanding his highest teaching. The *Memorabilia* therefore, in which Xenophon records his impressions of Socrates, is in the eyes of these scholars a very untrustworthy guide, and they maintain that in most of his works Plato does no more than preserve for posterity the content of Socrates' philosophy, without additions of his own. If so, it may be asked why a large number of Platonic dialogues show no trace of a disposition to grapple with difficult philosophical problems, and leave the reader with very much the same idea of Socratic teaching as do Xenophon's reminiscences, after making allowance for the infinitely greater charm of Plato as a writer. These dialogues are generally recognised as early works of Plato, and, inasmuch as they, together with the *Memorabilia* and the description of the individuality of Socrates, as it may be gathered from other Platonic writings, form one consistent whole, it seems reasonable to suppose that the philosophical developments found in such books as the *Republic* are due to Plato himself, and the independent expansion of his own genius.

The *Apology* is one of Plato's 'Socratic' works, as the early writings are usually termed. If it does not give us the exact words spoken by Socrates when on trial for his life, at any rate it represents their substance. The speech shows him to us in a very different light from the caricature in the *Clouds*. Convinced that he had a divine mission to rescue Athens from evil ways, and to set her on the road to amendment, he first tried to discover the source of her misdoing. This, as we have already seen, in the course of his hunt for a man wiser than himself, he declared to be her ignorance. In arts and crafts he saw that knowledge leads to right action, ignorance to failure. You cannot play an instrument well unless you learn how, you cannot be a chauffeur unless you know the working of motors, you cannot be a doctor unless you study medicine for several years. So far Athenians would agree with Socrates. 'But then,' he would argue, 'the art of living and governing rightly is far more difficult than any of these pursuits. How then can you Athenians maintain as you do that men can be virtuous and take part in politics without special training? In the professional arts ignorance means lack of skill; in the moral and political sphere it means vice. Ignorance is vice, virtue is knowledge.'

Socrates never believed that men erred otherwise than through ignorance. He knew that he himself had no difficulty in disciplining his will to do whatever his reason told him should be done. A clear understanding should show everyone that virtue alone produces the real welfare of mankind; therefore such a clear understanding should take away all disposition towards badness in any shape. He had an immense faith in human nature, thinking that no one would follow bad courses, if only a conviction of their harmfulness could be driven home.

Year in, year out, Socrates spent his days at Athens, trying to show the Athenians their sore need of knowledge. His usual method was to ask questions, professing ignorance himself, but always contriving to show the futility of ordinary notions of right and wrong. His skill in tearing to shreds definitions of piety, courage and the like, extracted from unwilling companions, no doubt roused hostility, but on the other hand he endeared himself to all the choicest spirits in Athens. He cherished a hope of training the most gifted among the Athenians to become seekers after truth, so that by the aid of their greater wisdom they might guide the general body of the citizens to better things.

How can the caricature in the *Clouds* bear any relation to the real Socrates with his moral earnestness? We must remember that his grotesque personal appearance and eccentric ways were too good a prey to be missed by any writer who wished to make game of the general spirit of enquiry into moral and scientific problems prevailing at the time in Athens. There were many people, going by the general name of Sophists, who professed to teach virtue, or showed the inadequacy of ordinarily accepted reasons for moral conduct, and these might easily be put along with Socrates for comic purposes. There were also many philosophers interested in natural science whom scoffers would be ready to ridicule. We learn from both Plato and Xenophon that Socrates too had been interested in these studies in his youth, although most scholars believe that he abandoned them in the hope of finding a more ready method whereby he might lead his fellows and himself to a better knowledge of virtue, and also because, as Plato tells us in the *Phaedo*, he was profoundly disappointed that the philosophers did little to explain and uphold the divine government of the universe. Such philosophers were apt to be very unorthodox in their religious views. It is therefore not surprising that Aristophanes should have dressed up in the guise of Socrates a figure embodying all the innovating movements of the time.

Socrates himself was a man of deeply religious temperament. Generally speaking, he talks of 'the gods' in the plural, and exhorts his countrymen to conform to the usual modes of worship, and also to consult oracles and use means of divination. But his belief rose to heights far above the conventional religion. It may be summed up as an unswerving faith in a Divine Reason, everywhere present in the universe, and ordering all for the good of man. The soul of man partakes in the divine, and in proportion as knowledge advances virtue will increase, and mankind will draw nearer to God.

Socrates believed that he possessed within himself a sure guide to prevent him from going astray. A 'divine sign' (δαιμόνιον σημεῖον) would often warn him against some intended action. The nature of this divine sign, often called simply δαιμόνιον, has been much discussed. Probably it was something very like what we call 'conscience', a sense of duty presenting itself to him so vividly that he seemed to hear a voice actually speaking and dissuading him from his purpose. Whatever it may have been, Socrates looked upon it as a special gift, granted to him and to few, if any, else of those who lived before him. In the *Apology*, 31 D, we are told that the δαιμόνιον only restrained and never urged him to any action. Sometimes the prohibition came on trivial occasions; sometimes it made a turning-point in his life, as when the voice prevented him from entering on an ordinary political career.

In another way also the mental experience of Socrates was abnormal. He was subject to trances, which might last for hours, even on one occasion for a whole day and night. During these seizures, he would stand motionless, and unconscious of everything about him, while his mind wrestled with some difficult thought.

Plato in the *Apology* reports Socrates as being brought to trial for the first time in his life at the age of 70. It is a matter of great difficulty to understand why, if the Athenians considered his presence in the city detrimental, an accusation should not have been brought against him long before 399 B.C. His manner of life had been the same for very many years. If the distress (ἀπορία) to which his hearers were reduced by his questions was the cause of hatred, that was no new thing. His habit of placing himself on a level with his interlocutors, however small their claim to intellectual or other merit, was no doubt often most irritating. Enemies called it εἰρωνεία, 'sly dissembling', but this same quality was seen by others in a different and truer light. His self-depreciation partly arose from real humility, and was partly due to playfulness and a humorous desire to avoid anything like a magisterial tone. As depicted by Plato, this trait seems the key to his lovableness, and, if it repelled some, it must surely have had much to do with the passionate attachment he inspired in his friends. He had all along denounced Athenian democracy and Athenian apathy towards everything that is most precious in life; his lack of religious orthodoxy was made the ground of the attack by Aristophanes four-and-twenty years before the actual trial. Were there then any additional motives that induced Anytus, a popular politician, by trade a rich tanner, Meletus, a hook-nosed, unknown young man (as Plato calls him in the *Euthyphro*), perhaps a poet or the son of a poet, and Lycon, a rhetorician of whom nothing is known, to bring an indictment against Socrates, in 399 B.C., accusing him of corrupting youth, failing to reverence the gods reverenced by the state, and introducing new divinities (δαιμόνια)?

Five years previously, after the downfall of Athens at the close of the Peloponnesian War, a body of irresponsible rulers, called the Thirty from their number, had been appointed by the orders of the Spartan general to administer affairs at Athens. For eight months the Thirty reigned in the city, to the terror of the inhabitants, large numbers of whom fled to Thebes and elsewhere. Socrates was not amongst those who left Athens. Though he had refused at the peril of his life (*Apology*, 32 D) to obey a tyrannical order of the Thirty, yet several of his associates, especially Critias, the most prominent of the Thirty, and Alcibiades, had been anti-democratic, and Socrates' own attitude of criticism towards Athenian institutions was notorious. Accordingly when the voluntary exiles returned, drove out the Thirty, and restored the democracy on the old lines, Socrates was more than ever eyed askance. But an amnesty had been granted to all persons who had been against democracy except to the Thirty themselves and a very few others. Socrates could not therefore be prosecuted on political grounds, and some other cause of offence had to be sought by his enemies, whom we may with good reason suppose to have been chiefly moved by his slighting opinion of Athenian democratic institutions, such as election by lot, and by the fear that his teaching would produce an oligarchical spirit among young men in the future, as it had done in the past.

Thus the main accusation against Socrates was the charge of corrupting youth. Recently attempts have been made to prove that the 'new δαιμόνια' of whose introduction the indictment accuses him have no reference to his δαιμόνιον, or 'divine sign'. These efforts to discredit the statements of Plato to the contrary in the *Apology*, 31 D, and *Euthyphro*, 3 B, seem to me unsuccessful, though it would take too much space to give the reasons here. In any case, however, it seems clear that the 'new divinities' were not the chief cause of the attack, and Socrates was probably not condemned on this score. Professor Burnet gives an interesting conjectural explanation of the reason why many more of the jury voted for the death than had voted for the condemnation of Socrates. Not only the defiant attitude of the defendant in his second speech, chapters xxv–xxviii, roused their wrath, but 'everything becomes clear if we suppose that the real ground of the accusation could not for some reason be stated in the indictment, and that some of the judges thought it unfair to condemn a man for an offence with which he was not formally charged, even though they might believe him guilty of it'.[1] After condemnation these jurors may very probably have no longer hesitated to vote for the extreme penalty.

We can only guess at the substance of the speeches for the prosecution. Some evidence from the *Memorabilia* of Xenophon tends to show that the attack was far more serious on the side of the dangerous tendencies in the civic teaching of Socrates than as regards his alleged impiety. From the *Apology* also we see that Meletus came to grief in his endeavour to establish the charge of atheism. Nevertheless, in spite of the noble speech for the defence a verdict of guilty was returned by a majority of sixty-one votes in a court of 501 jurors. The accusers then proposed the penalty of death. In cases of this kind the defendant was allowed to propose an alternative penalty. Between these two, and these two only, the court might choose. With difficulty Socrates was persuaded by his friends to propose a fine of about £120, which they undertook to pay. This seems to have been

[1] *Greek Philosophy*, *Thales to Plato*, p. 186.

thought so inadequate as to show contempt of court, and eighty more jurors (according to a late account of the trial) voted for the death sentence.

One month elapsed between the trial and the death of Socrates. It was the time of a great annual festival at the island of Delos, to which Athens used regularly to send a sacred ship. No capital punishment might pollute the city during the absence of the ship. While waiting for her return Socrates was in prison for thirty days, spending the time in serene converse with his friends, and, as we should expect from the *Apology*, utterly unperturbed in the face of death. The *Phaedo* of Plato gives us the last scene. We are told that the ship had arrived the day before, and Socrates was to drink at sundown the cup of hemlock appointed for his death. From earliest dawn till the close of the day the talk went on as usual, combining tender playfulness with high discourse on death as the release of the Soul from her prison-house, the body. When the hour came, Socrates maintained his perfect calmness to the last, strong in his conviction that only after death will the lover of Wisdom meet her in her purity.

ΑΠΟΛΟΓΙΑ ΣΩΚΡΑΤΟΥΣ

PART I. BEFORE THE VERDICT

(First Speech)

CHAPTERS I–XXIV

INTRODUCTION: I–II

17   I. Ὅ τι μὲν ὑμεῖς, ὦ ἄνδρες Ἀθηναῖοι, πεπόνθατε
ὑπὸ τῶν ἐμῶν κατηγόρων, οὐκ οἶδα· ἐγὼ δ᾽ οὖν καὶ
αὐτὸς ὑπ᾽ αὐτῶν ὀλίγου ἐμαυτοῦ ἐπελαθόμην· οὕτω
πιθανῶς ἔλεγον. καί τοι ἀληθές γε, ὡς ἔπος εἰπεῖν,
οὐδὲν εἰρήκασιν. μάλιστα δὲ αὐτῶν ἓν ἐθαύμασα τῶν 5
πολλῶν ὧν ἐψεύσαντο, τοῦτο ἐν ᾧ ἔλεγον ὡς χρὴ
ὑμᾶς εὐλαβεῖσθαι, μὴ ὑπ᾽ ἐμοῦ ἐξαπατηθῆτε, ὡς
B δεινοῦ ὄντος λέγειν. τὸ γὰρ μὴ αἰσχυνθῆναι, ὅτι
αὐτίκα ὑπ᾽ ἐμοῦ ἐξελεγχθήσονται ἔργῳ, ἐπειδὰν μηδ᾽
ὁπωστιοῦν φαίνωμαι δεινὸς λέγειν, τοῦτό μοι ἔδοξεν 10
αὐτῶν ἀναισχυντότατον εἶναι, εἰ μὴ ἄρα δεινὸν
καλοῦσιν οὗτοι λέγειν τὸν τἀληθῆ λέγοντα· εἰ μὲν γὰρ
τοῦτο λέγουσιν, ὁμολογοίην ἂν ἔγωγε οὐ κατὰ τούτους
εἶναι ῥήτωρ. οὗτοι μὲν οὖν, ὥσπερ ἐγὼ λέγω, ἤ τι ἢ
οὐδὲν ἀληθὲς εἰρήκασιν· ὑμεῖς δέ μου ἀκούσεσθε 15
πᾶσαν τὴν ἀλήθειαν. οὐ μέντοι μὰ Δία, ὦ ἄνδρες
Ἀθηναῖοι, κεκαλλιεπημένους γε λόγους, ὥσπερ οἱ
C τούτων, ῥήμασί τε καὶ ὀνόμασιν, οὐδὲ κεκοσμημένους,
ἀλλ᾽ ἀκούσεσθε εἰκῇ λεγόμενα τοῖς ἐπιτυχοῦσιν
ὀνόμασιν· πιστεύω γὰρ δίκαια εἶναι ἃ λέγω, καὶ 20
μηδεὶς ὑμῶν προσδοκησάτω ἄλλως· οὐδὲ γὰρ ἂν

20

δήπου πρέποι, ὦ ἄνδρες, τῇδε τῇ ἡλικίᾳ ὥσπερ
μειρακίῳ πλάττοντι λόγους εἰς ὑμᾶς εἰσιέναι. καὶ
μέντοι καὶ πάνυ, ὦ ἄνδρες Ἀθηναῖοι, τοῦτο ὑμῶν
δέομαι καὶ παρίεμαι· ἐὰν διὰ τῶν αὐτῶν λόγων 25
ἀκούητέ μου ἀπολογουμένου, δι' ὧνπερ εἴωθα λέγειν
καὶ ἐν ἀγορᾷ ἐπὶ τῶν τραπεζῶν, ἵνα ὑμῶν πολλοὶ
D ἀκηκόασι, καὶ ἄλλοθι, μήτε θαυμάζειν μήτε θορυβεῖν
τούτου ἕνεκα. ἔχει γὰρ οὑτωσί. νῦν ἐγὼ πρῶτον ἐπὶ
δικαστήριον ἀναβέβηκα, ἔτη γεγονὼς ἑβδομήκοντα· 30
ἀτεχνῶς οὖν ξένως ἔχω τῆς ἐνθάδε λέξεως. ὥσπερ
οὖν ἄν, εἰ τῷ ὄντι ξένος ἐτύγχανον ὤν, ξυνεγιγνώσκετε δήπου ἄν μοι, εἰ ἐν ἐκείνῃ τῇ φωνῇ τε καὶ τῷ
18 τρόπῳ ἔλεγον, ἐν | οἷσπερ ἐτεθράμμην, καὶ δὴ καὶ νῦν
τοῦτο ὑμῶν δέομαι δίκαιον, ὥς γέ μοι δοκῶ, τὸν μὲν 35
τρόπον τῆς λέξεως ἐᾶν· ἴσως μὲν γὰρ χείρων, ἴσως δὲ
βελτίων ἂν εἴη· αὐτὸ δὲ τοῦτο σκοπεῖν καὶ τούτῳ τὸν
νοῦν προσέχειν, εἰ δίκαια λέγω ἢ μή· δικαστοῦ μὲν
γὰρ αὕτη ἀρετή, ῥήτορος δὲ τἀληθῆ λέγειν.

II. Πρῶτον μὲν οὖν δίκαιός εἰμι ἀπολογήσασθαι, ὦ
ἄνδρες Ἀθηναῖοι, πρὸς τὰ πρῶτά μου ψεύδη κατηγορημένα καὶ τοὺς πρώτους κατηγόρους, ἔπειτα δὲ πρὸς
B τὰ ὕστερα καὶ τοὺς ὑστέρους. ἐμοῦ γὰρ πολλοὶ
κατήγοροι γεγόνασιν πρὸς ὑμᾶς καὶ πάλαι, πολλὰ 5
ἤδη ἔτη καὶ οὐδὲν ἀληθὲς λέγοντες, οὓς ἐγὼ μᾶλλον
φοβοῦμαι ἢ τοὺς ἀμφὶ Ἄνυτον, καίπερ ὄντας καὶ
τούτους δεινούς· ἀλλ' ἐκεῖνοι δεινότεροι, ὦ ἄνδρες, οἳ
ὑμῶν τοὺς πολλοὺς ἐκ παίδων παραλαμβάνοντες
ἔπειθόν τε καὶ κατηγόρουν ἐμοῦ [μᾶλλον] οὐδὲν 10
ἀληθές, ὡς ἔστιν τις Σωκράτης, σοφὸς ἀνήρ, τά τε μετέωρα φροντιστὴς καὶ τὰ ὑπὸ γῆς ἅπαντα ἀνεζητηκὼς

καὶ τὸν ἥττω λόγον κρείττω ποιῶν. οὗτοι, ὦ ἄνδρες
c Ἀθηναῖοι, οἱ ταύτην τὴν φήμην κατασκεδάσαντες,
οἱ δεινοί εἰσίν μου κατήγοροι· οἱ γὰρ ἀκούοντες 15
ἡγοῦνται τοὺς ταῦτα ζητοῦντας οὐδὲ θεοὺς νομίζειν.
ἔπειτά εἰσιν οὗτοι οἱ κατήγοροι πολλοὶ καὶ πολὺν
χρόνον ἤδη κατηγορηκότες, ἔτι δὲ καὶ ἐν ταύτῃ τῇ
ἡλικίᾳ λέγοντες πρὸς ὑμᾶς, ἐν ᾗ ἂν μάλιστα ἐπιστεύσατε, παῖδες ὄντες, ἔνιοι δ' ὑμῶν καὶ μειράκια, ἀτεχνῶς 20
ἐρήμην κατηγοροῦντες ἀπολογουμένου οὐδενός. ὃ δὲ
πάντων ἀλογώτατον, ὅτι οὐδὲ τὰ ὀνόματα οἷόν τε
d αὐτῶν εἰδέναι καὶ εἰπεῖν, πλὴν εἴ τις κωμῳδοποιὸς
τυγχάνει ὤν· ὅσοι δὲ φθόνῳ καὶ διαβολῇ χρώμενοι
ὑμᾶς ἀνέπειθον, οἱ δὲ καὶ αὐτοὶ πεπεισμένοι ἄλλους 25
πείθοντες, οὗτοι πάντες ἀπορώτατοί εἰσιν· οὐδὲ γὰρ
ἀναβιβάσασθαι οἷόν τ' ἐστὶν αὐτῶν ἐνταυθοῖ οὐδ'
ἐλέγξαι οὐδένα, ἀλλ' ἀνάγκη ἀτεχνῶς ὥσπερ σκια-
μαχεῖν ἀπολογούμενόν τε καὶ ἐλέγχειν μηδενὸς ἀπο-
κρινομένου. ἀξιώσατε οὖν καὶ ὑμεῖς, ὥσπερ ἐγὼ λέγω, 30
διττούς μου τοὺς κατηγόρους γεγονέναι, ἑτέρους μὲν
e τοὺς ἄρτι κατηγορήσαντας, ἑτέρους δὲ τοὺς πάλαι, οὓς
ἐγὼ λέγω, καὶ οἰήθητε δεῖν πρὸς ἐκείνους πρῶτόν με
ἀπολογήσασθαι· καὶ γὰρ ὑμεῖς ἐκείνων πρότερον
ἠκούσατε κατηγορούντων, καὶ πολὺ μᾶλλον ἢ τῶνδε 35
τῶν ὕστερον. εἶεν· ἀπολογητέον δή, ὦ ἄνδρες
19 Ἀθηναῖοι, καὶ ἐπιχειρητέον | ὑμῶν ἐξελέσθαι τὴν δια-
βολήν, ἣν ὑμεῖς ἐν πολλῷ χρόνῳ ἔσχετε, ταύτην ἐν
οὕτως ὀλίγῳ χρόνῳ. βουλοίμην μὲν οὖν ἂν τοῦτο
οὕτως γενέσθαι, εἴ τι ἄμεινον καὶ ὑμῖν καὶ ἐμοί, καὶ 40
πλέον τί με ποιῆσαι ἀπολογούμενον· οἶμαι δὲ αὐτὸ
χαλεπὸν εἶναι, καὶ οὐ πάνυ με λανθάνει οἷόν ἐστιν.

ὅμως τοῦτο μὲν ἴτω ὅπη τῷ θεῷ φίλον, τῷ δὲ νόμῳ
πειστέον καὶ ἀπολογητέον.

SOCRATES DEFENDS HIMSELF AGAINST
THE πρῶτοι κατήγοροι: III–X

III. Ἀναλάβωμεν οὖν ἐξ ἀρχῆς, τίς ἡ κατηγορία
B ἐστίν, ἐξ ἧς ἡ ἐμὴ διαβολὴ γέγονεν, ᾗ δὴ καὶ πιστεύων
Μέλητός με ἐγράψατο τὴν γραφὴν ταύτην. εἶεν· τί δὴ
λέγοντες διέβαλλον οἱ διαβάλλοντες; ὥσπερ οὖν
κατηγόρων τὴν ἀντωμοσίαν δεῖ ἀναγνῶναι αὐτῶν· 5
"Σωκράτης ἀδικεῖ καὶ περιεργάζεται ζητῶν τά τε ὑπὸ
γῆς καὶ οὐράνια καὶ τὸν ἥττω λόγον κρείττω ποιῶν
C καὶ ἄλλους τὰ αὐτὰ ταῦτα διδάσκων." τοιαύτη τίς
ἐστιν· ταῦτα γὰρ ἑωρᾶτε καὶ αὐτοὶ ἐν τῇ Ἀριστο-
φάνους κωμῳδίᾳ, Σωκράτη τινὰ ἐκεῖ περιφερόμενον, 10
φάσκοντά τε ἀεροβατεῖν καὶ ἄλλην πολλὴν φλυαρίαν
φλυαροῦντα, ὧν ἐγὼ οὐδὲν οὔτε μέγα οὔτε μικρὸν πέρι
ἐπαΐω. καὶ οὐχ ὡς ἀτιμάζων λέγω τὴν τοιαύτην
ἐπιστήμην, εἴ τις περὶ τῶν τοιούτων σοφός ἐστιν· μή
πως ἐγὼ ὑπὸ Μελήτου τοσαύτας δίκας φύγοιμι· ἀλλὰ 15
D γὰρ ἐμοὶ τούτων, ὦ ἄνδρες Ἀθηναῖοι, οὐδὲν μέτεστιν·
μάρτυρας δὲ αὐτοὺς ὑμῶν τοὺς πολλοὺς παρέχομαι,
καὶ ἀξιῶ ὑμᾶς ἀλλήλους διδάσκειν τε καὶ φράζειν,
ὅσοι ἐμοῦ πώποτε ἀκηκόατε διαλεγομένου· πολλοὶ δὲ
ὑμῶν οἱ τοιοῦτοί εἰσιν· φράζετε οὖν ἀλλήλοις, εἰ 20
πώποτε ἢ μικρὸν ἢ μέγα ἤκουσέ τις ὑμῶν ἐμοῦ περὶ
τῶν τοιούτων διαλεγομένου· καὶ ἐκ τούτων γνώσεσθε
ὅτι τοιαῦτ' ἐστὶν καὶ τἆλλα περὶ ἐμοῦ ἃ οἱ πολλοὶ
λέγουσιν.

IV. Ἀλλὰ γὰρ οὔτε τούτων οὐδέν ἐστιν, οὐδέ γ' εἴ
τινος ἀκηκόατε ὡς ἐγὼ παιδεύειν ἐπιχειρῶ ἀνθρώπους
E καὶ χρήματα πράττομαι, οὐδὲ τοῦτο ἀληθές. ἐπεὶ καὶ
τοῦτό γέ μοι δοκεῖ καλὸν εἶναι, εἴ τις οἷός τ' εἴη
παιδεύειν ἀνθρώπους ὥσπερ Γοργίας τε ὁ Λεοντῖνος 5
καὶ Πρόδικος ὁ Κεῖος καὶ Ἱππίας ὁ Ἠλεῖος. τούτων
γὰρ ἕκαστος, ὦ ἄνδρες, οἷός τ' ἐστὶν ἰὼν εἰς ἑκάστην
τῶν πόλεων τοὺς νέους, οἷς ἔξεστι τῶν ἑαυτῶν
πολιτῶν προῖκα ξυνεῖναι ᾧ ἂν βούλωνται,—τούτους
20 πείθουσι τὰς ἐκείνων ξυνουσίας | ἀπολιπόντας σφίσιν 10
ξυνεῖναι χρήματα διδόντας καὶ χάριν προσειδέναι.
ἐπεὶ καὶ ἄλλος ἀνήρ ἐστι Πάριος ἐνθάδε σοφός, ὃν
ἐγὼ ᾐσθόμην ἐπιδημοῦντα· ἔτυχον γὰρ προσελθὼν
ἀνδρὶ ὃς τετέλεκε χρήματα σοφισταῖς πλείω ἢ
ξύμπαντες οἱ ἄλλοι, Καλλίᾳ τῷ Ἱππονίκου· τοῦτον 15
οὖν ἀνηρόμην—ἐστὸν γὰρ αὐτῷ δύο υἱέε—Ὦ Καλλία,
ἦν δ' ἐγώ, εἰ μέν σου τὼ υἱέε πώλω ἢ μόσχω ἐγενέσθην,
εἴχομεν ἂν αὐτοῖν ἐπιστάτην λαβεῖν καὶ μισθώσασθαι,
B ὃς ἔμελλεν αὐτὼ καλώ τε κἀγαθὼ ποιήσειν τὴν
προσήκουσαν ἀρετήν· ἦν δ' ἂν οὗτος ἢ τῶν ἱππικῶν τις ἢ 20
τῶν γεωργικῶν· νῦν δ' ἐπειδὴ ἀνθρώπω ἐστόν, τίνα
αὐτοῖν ἐν νῷ ἔχεις ἐπιστάτην λαβεῖν; τίς τῆς τοιαύτης
ἀρετῆς, τῆς ἀνθρωπίνης τε καὶ πολιτικῆς, ἐπιστήμων
ἐστίν; οἶμαι γάρ σε ἐσκέφθαι διὰ τὴν τῶν υἱέων
κτῆσιν. ἔστιν τις, ἔφην ἐγώ, ἢ οὔ; Πάνυ γε, ἦ δ' ὅς. 25
Τίς, ἦν δ' ἐγώ, καὶ ποδαπός, καὶ πόσου διδάσκει;
Εὔηνος, ἔφη, ὦ Σώκρατες, Πάριος, πέντε μνῶν· καὶ
ἐγὼ τὸν Εὔηνον ἐμακάρισα, εἰ ὡς ἀληθῶς ἔχοι ταύτην
C τὴν τέχνην καὶ οὕτως ἐμμελῶς διδάσκοι. ἐγὼ οὖν
καὶ αὐτὸς ἐκαλλυνόμην τε καὶ ἡβρυνόμην ἄν, εἰ 30

ἠπιστάμην ταῦτα· ἀλλ' οὐ γὰρ ἐπίσταμαι, ὦ ἄνδρες
Ἀθηναῖοι.

V. Ὑπολάβοι ἂν οὖν τις ὑμῶν ἴσως· Ἀλλ', ὦ
Σώκρατες, τὸ σὸν τί ἐστι πρᾶγμα; πόθεν αἱ διαβολαί
σοι αὗται γεγόνασιν; οὐ γὰρ δήπου σοῦ γε οὐδὲν τῶν
ἄλλων περιττότερον πραγματευομένου ἔπειτα τοσαύτη
φήμη τε καὶ λόγος γέγονεν, εἰ μή τι ἔπραττες ἀλλοῖον 5
D ἢ οἱ πολλοί· λέγε οὖν ἡμῖν, τί ἐστιν, ἵνα μὴ ἡμεῖς περὶ
σοῦ αὐτοσχεδιάζωμεν. ταυτί μοι δοκεῖ δίκαια λέγειν
ὁ λέγων, κἀγὼ ὑμῖν πειράσομαι ἀποδεῖξαι, τί ποτ'
ἔστιν τοῦτο ὃ ἐμοὶ πεποίηκε τό τε ὄνομα καὶ τὴν
διαβολήν. ἀκούετε δή. καὶ ἴσως μὲν δόξω τισὶν 10
ὑμῶν παίζειν, εὖ μέντοι ἴστε, πᾶσαν ὑμῖν τὴν ἀλήθειαν
ἐρῶ. ἐγὼ γάρ, ὦ ἄνδρες Ἀθηναῖοι, δι' οὐδὲν ἀλλ' ἢ
διὰ σοφίαν τινὰ τοῦτο τὸ ὄνομα ἔσχηκα. ποίαν δὴ
σοφίαν ταύτην; ἥπερ ἐστὶν ἴσως ἀνθρωπίνη σοφία. τῷ
ὄντι γὰρ κινδυνεύω ταύτην εἶναι σοφός· οὗτοι δὲ τάχ' 15
E ἄν, οὓς ἄρτι ἔλεγον, μείζω τινὰ ἢ κατ' ἄνθρωπον
σοφίαν σοφοὶ εἶεν, ἢ οὐκ ἔχω τί λέγω· οὐ γὰρ δὴ
ἔγωγε αὐτὴν ἐπίσταμαι, ἀλλ' ὅστις φησὶ ψεύδεταί τε
καὶ ἐπὶ διαβολῇ τῇ ἐμῇ λέγει. καί μοι, ὦ ἄνδρες
Ἀθηναῖοι, μὴ θορυβήσητε, μηδὲ ἂν δόξω τι ὑμῖν μέγα 20
λέγειν· οὐ γὰρ ἐμὸν ἐρῶ τὸν λόγον, ὃν ἂν λέγω, ἀλλ'
εἰς ἀξιόχρεων ὑμῖν τὸν λέγοντα ἀνοίσω. τῆς γὰρ ἐμῆς,
εἰ δή τίς ἐστι σοφία καὶ οἵα, μάρτυρα ὑμῖν παρέξομαι
τὸν θεὸν τὸν ἐν Δελφοῖς. Χαιρεφῶντα γὰρ ἴστε που.
21 οὗτος | ἐμός τε ἑταῖρος ἦν ἐκ νέου, καὶ ὑμῶν τῷ 25
πλήθει ἑταῖρός τε καὶ ξυνέφυγε τὴν φυγὴν ταύτην καὶ
μεθ' ὑμῶν κατῆλθε. καὶ ἴστε δὴ οἷος ἦν Χαιρεφῶν, ὡς
φοοδρὸς ἐφ' ὅ τι ὁρμήσειεν. καὶ δή ποτε καὶ εἰς

Δελφοὺς ἐλθὼν ἐτόλμησε τοῦτο μαντεύσασθαι· καί, ὅπερ λέγω, μὴ θορυβεῖτε, ὦ ἄνδρες· ἤρετο γὰρ δή, εἴ 30 τις ἐμοῦ εἴη σοφώτερος. ἀνεῖλεν οὖν ἡ Πυθία μηδένα σοφώτερον εἶναι. καὶ τούτων πέρι ὁ ἀδελφὸς ὑμῖν αὐτοῦ οὑτοσὶ μαρτυρήσει, ἐπειδὴ ἐκεῖνος τετελεύτηκεν.

B VI. Σκέψασθε δὲ ὧν ἕνεκα ταῦτα λέγω· μέλλω γὰρ ὑμᾶς διδάξειν, ὅθεν μοι ἡ διαβολὴ γέγονε. ταῦτα γὰρ ἐγὼ ἀκούσας ἐνεθυμούμην οὑτωσί· Τί ποτε λέγει ὁ θεός, καὶ τί ποτε αἰνίττεται; ἐγὼ γὰρ δὴ οὔτε μέγα οὔτε σμικρὸν ξύνοιδα ἐμαυτῷ σοφὸς ὤν· τί οὖν ποτὲ 5 λέγει φάσκων ἐμὲ σοφώτατον εἶναι; οὐ γὰρ δήπου ψεύδεταί γε· οὐ γὰρ θέμις αὐτῷ. καὶ πολὺν μὲν χρόνον ἠπόρουν, τί ποτε λέγει, ἔπειτα μόγις πάνυ ἐπὶ ζήτησιν αὐτοῦ τοιαύτην τινὰ ἐτραπόμην. ἦλθον ἐπί

C τινα τῶν δοκούντων σοφῶν εἶναι, ὡς ἐνταῦθα, εἴ πέρ 10 που, ἐλέγξων τὸ μαντεῖον καὶ ἀποφανῶν τῷ χρησμῷ ὅτι Οὑτοσὶ ἐμοῦ σοφώτερός ἐστι, σὺ δ' ἐμὲ ἔφησθα. διασκοπῶν οὖν τοῦτον—ὀνόματι γὰρ οὐδὲν δέομαι λέγειν, ἦν δέ τις τῶν πολιτικῶν πρὸς ὃν ἐγὼ σκοπῶν τοιοῦτόν τι ἔπαθον, ὦ ἄνδρες Ἀθηναῖοι—καὶ δια- 15 λεγόμενος αὐτῷ, ἔδοξέ μοι οὗτος ὁ ἀνὴρ δοκεῖν μὲν εἶναι σοφὸς ἄλλοις τε πολλοῖς ἀνθρώποις καὶ μάλιστα ἑαυτῷ, εἶναι δ' οὔ. κἄπειτα ἐπειρώμην αὐτῷ δεικ-

D νύναι, ὅτι οἴοιτο μὲν εἶναι σοφός, εἴη δ' οὔ. ἐντεῦθεν οὖν τούτῳ τε ἀπηχθόμην καὶ πολλοῖς τῶν παρόντων, 20 πρὸς ἐμαυτὸν δ' οὖν ἀπιὼν ἐλογιζόμην ὅτι τούτου μὲν τοῦ ἀνθρώπου ἐγὼ σοφώτερός εἰμι· κινδυνεύει μὲν γὰρ ἡμῶν οὐδέτερος οὐδὲν καλὸν κἀγαθὸν εἰδέναι, ἀλλ' οὗτος μὲν οἴεταί τι εἰδέναι οὐκ εἰδώς, ἐγὼ δέ, ὥσπερ οὖν οὐκ οἶδα, οὐδὲ οἴομαι· ἔοικα γοῦν τούτου γε 25

σμικρῷ τινι αὐτῷ τούτῳ σοφώτερος εἶναι, ὅτι ἃ μὴ
οἶδα οὐδὲ οἴομαι εἰδέναι. ἐντεῦθεν ἐπ᾽ ἄλλον ᾖα τῶν
E ἐκείνου δοκούντων σοφωτέρων εἶναι, καί μοι ταὐτὰ
ταῦτα ἔδοξε. καὶ ἐνταῦθα κἀκείνῳ καὶ ἄλλοις πολλοῖς
ἀπηχθόμην.   30

VII. Μετὰ ταῦτ᾽ οὖν ἤδη ἐφεξῆς ᾖα, αἰσθανόμενος
μὲν καὶ λυπούμενος καὶ δεδιὼς ὅτι ἀπηχθανόμην,
ὅμως δὲ ἀναγκαῖον ἐδόκει εἶναι τὸ τοῦ θεοῦ περὶ
πλείστου ποιεῖσθαι· ἰτέον οὖν σκοποῦντι τὸν χρησμόν,
τί λέγει, ἐπὶ ἅπαντας τούς τι δοκοῦντας εἰδέναι. καὶ 5
22 νὴ τὸν κύνα, ὦ ἄνδρες | Ἀθηναῖοι· δεῖ γὰρ πρὸς ὑμᾶς
τἀληθῆ λέγειν· ἦ μὴν ἐγὼ ἔπαθόν τι τοιοῦτον· οἱ μὲν
μάλιστα εὐδοκιμοῦντες ἔδοξάν μοι ὀλίγου δεῖν τοῦ
πλείστου ἐνδεεῖς εἶναι ζητοῦντι κατὰ τὸν θεόν, ἄλλοι
δὲ δοκοῦντες φαυλότεροι ἐπιεικέστεροι εἶναι ἄνδρες 10
πρὸς τὸ φρονίμως ἔχειν. δεῖ δὴ ὑμῖν τὴν ἐμὴν πλάνην
ἐπιδεῖξαι ὥσπερ πόνους τινὰς πονοῦντος, ἵνα μοι καὶ
ἀνέλεγκτος ἡ μαντεία γένοιτο. μετὰ γὰρ τοὺς πολιτι-
κοὺς ᾖα ἐπὶ τοὺς ποιητὰς τούς τε τῶν τραγῳδιῶν καὶ
B τοὺς τῶν διθυράμβων καὶ τοὺς ἄλλους, ὡς ἐνταῦθα ἐπ᾽ 15
αὐτοφώρῳ καταληψόμενος ἐμαυτὸν ἀμαθέστερον ἐκείνων ὄντα. ἀναλαμβάνων οὖν αὐτῶν τὰ ποιήματα, ἃ
μοι ἐδόκει μάλιστα πεπραγματεῦσθαι αὐτοῖς, διηρώτων
ἂν αὐτοὺς τί λέγοιεν, ἵν᾽ ἅμα τι καὶ μανθάνοιμι παρ᾽
αὐτῶν. αἰσχύνομαι οὖν ὑμῖν εἰπεῖν, ὦ ἄνδρες, τἀληθῆ, 20
ὅμως δὲ ῥητέον. ὡς ἔπος γὰρ εἰπεῖν ὀλίγου αὐτῶν
ἅπαντες οἱ παρόντες ἂν βέλτιον ἔλεγον περὶ ὧν αὐτοὶ
C ἐπεποιήκεσαν. ἔγνων οὖν καὶ περὶ τῶν ποιητῶν ἐν
ὀλίγῳ τοῦτο, ὅτι οὐ σοφίᾳ ποιοῖεν, ἃ ποιοῖεν, ἀλλὰ
φύσει τινὶ καὶ ἐνθουσιάζοντες, ὥσπερ οἱ θεομάντεις καὶ 25

οἱ χρησμῳδοί· καὶ γὰρ οὗτοι λέγουσι μὲν πολλὰ καὶ
καλά, ἴσασιν δὲ οὐδὲν ὧν λέγουσι. τοιοῦτόν τί μοι
ἐφάνησαν πάθος καὶ οἱ ποιηταὶ πεπονθότες· καὶ ἅμα
ᾐσθόμην αὐτῶν διὰ τὴν ποίησιν οἰομένων καὶ τἆλλα
σοφωτάτων εἶναι ἀνθρώπων ἃ οὐκ ἦσαν. ἀπῇα οὖν καὶ 30
ἐντεῦθεν τῷ αὐτῷ οἰόμενος περιγεγονέναι, ᾧπερ καὶ
τῶν πολιτικῶν.

VIII. Τελευτῶν οὖν ἐπὶ τοὺς χειροτέχνας ᾖα·
D ἐμαυτῷ γὰρ ξυνῄδη οὐδὲν ἐπισταμένῳ, ὡς ἔπος
εἰπεῖν, τούτους δέ γ᾽ ᾔδη ὅτι εὑρήσοιμι πολλὰ καὶ
καλὰ ἐπισταμένους. καὶ τούτου μὲν οὐκ ἐψεύσθην,
ἀλλ᾽ ἠπίσταντο ἃ ἐγὼ οὐκ ἠπιστάμην καί μου ταύτῃ 5
σοφώτεροι ἦσαν. ἀλλ᾽, ὦ ἄνδρες Ἀθηναῖοι, ταὐτόν μοι
ἔδοξαν ἔχειν ἁμάρτημα, ὅπερ καὶ οἱ ποιηταί, καὶ οἱ
ἀγαθοὶ δημιουργοί· διὰ τὸ τὴν τέχνην καλῶς ἐξεργάζ-
εσθαι ἕκαστος ἠξίου καὶ τἆλλα τὰ μέγιστα σοφώτατος
εἶναι, καὶ αὐτῶν αὕτη ἡ πλημμέλεια ἐκείνην τὴν 10
E σοφίαν ἀπέκρυπτεν· ὥστε με ἐμαυτὸν ἀνερωτᾶν ὑπὲρ
τοῦ χρησμοῦ, πότερα δεξαίμην ἂν οὕτως ὥσπερ ἔχω
ἔχειν, μήτε τι σοφὸς ὢν τὴν ἐκείνων σοφίαν, μήτε
ἀμαθὴς τὴν ἀμαθίαν, ἢ ἀμφότερα ἃ ἐκεῖνοι ἔχουσιν
ἔχειν. ἀπεκρινάμην οὖν ἐμαυτῷ καὶ τῷ χρησμῷ, ὅτι 15
μοι λυσιτελοῖ ὥσπερ ἔχω ἔχειν.

IX. Ἐκ ταυτησὶ δὴ τῆς ἐξετάσεως, ὦ ἄνδρες
23 Ἀθηναῖοι, πολλαὶ μὲν ἀπέχθειαί μοι γεγόνασι | καὶ
οἷαι χαλεπώταται καὶ βαρύταται, ὥστε πολλὰς διαβολὰς ἀπ᾽ αὐτῶν γεγονέναι, ὄνομα δὲ τοῦτο λέγεσθαι,
σοφὸς εἶναι. οἴονται γάρ με ἑκάστοτε οἱ παρόντες 5
ταῦτα αὐτὸν εἶναι σοφόν, ἃ ἂν ἄλλον ἐξελέγξω· τὸ δὲ
κινδυνεύει, ὦ ἄνδρες, τῷ ὄντι ὁ θεὸς σοφὸς εἶναι, καὶ

ἐν τῷ χρησμῷ τούτῳ τοῦτο λέγειν, ὅτι ἡ ἀνθρωπίνη
σοφία ὀλίγου τινὸς ἀξία ἐστὶ καὶ οὐδενός. καὶ φαίνεται τοῦτ' οὐ λέγειν τὸν Σωκράτη, προσκεχρῆσθαι δὲ 10
B τῷ ἐμῷ ὀνόματι, ἐμὲ παράδειγμα ποιούμενος, ὥσπερ
ἂν εἰ εἴποι ὅτι Οὗτος ὑμῶν, ὦ ἄνθρωποι, σοφώτατός
ἐστιν, ὅστις ὥσπερ Σωκράτης ἔγνωκεν ὅτι οὐδενὸς
ἄξιός ἐστι τῇ ἀληθείᾳ πρὸς σοφίαν. ταῦτ' οὖν ἐγὼ
μὲν ἔτι καὶ νῦν περιιὼν ζητῶ καὶ ἐρευνῶ κατὰ τὸν 15
θεόν, καὶ τῶν ἀστῶν καὶ ξένων ἄν τινα οἴωμαι σοφὸν
εἶναι· καὶ ἐπειδάν μοι μὴ δοκῇ, τῷ θεῷ βοηθῶν
ἐνδείκνυμαι ὅτι οὐκ ἔστι σοφός. καὶ ὑπὸ ταύτης τῆς
ἀσχολίας οὔτε τι τῶν τῆς πόλεως πρᾶξαί μοι σχολὴ
C γέγονεν ἄξιον λόγου οὔτε τῶν οἰκείων, ἀλλ' ἐν πενίᾳ 20
μυρίᾳ εἰμὶ διὰ τὴν τοῦ θεοῦ λατρείαν.

X. Πρὸς δὲ τούτοις οἱ νέοι μοι ἐπακολουθοῦντες οἷς
μάλιστα σχολή ἐστιν, οἱ τῶν πλουσιωτάτων, αὐτόματοι, χαίρουσιν ἀκούοντες ἐξεταζομένων τῶν ἀνθρώπων, καὶ αὐτοὶ πολλάκις ἐμὲ μιμοῦνται, εἶτα
ἐπιχειροῦσιν ἄλλους ἐξετάζειν· κἄπειτα, οἶμαι, εὑρί- 5
σκουσι πολλὴν ἀφθονίαν οἰομένων μὲν εἰδέναι τι
ἀνθρώπων, εἰδότων δὲ ὀλίγα ἢ οὐδέν. ἐντεῦθεν
οὖν οἱ ὑπ' αὐτῶν ἐξεταζόμενοι ἐμοὶ ὀργίζονται, ἀλλ'
D οὐχ αὑτοῖς, καὶ λέγουσιν ὡς Σωκράτης τίς ἐστι
μιαρώτατος καὶ διαφθείρει τοὺς νέους· καὶ ἐπειδάν 10
τις αὐτοὺς ἐρωτᾷ, ὅ τι ποιῶν καὶ ὅ τι διδάσκων,
ἔχουσι μὲν οὐδὲν εἰπεῖν, ἀλλ' ἀγνοοῦσιν, ἵνα δὲ μὴ
δοκῶσιν ἀπορεῖν, τὰ κατὰ πάντων τῶν φιλοσοφούντων
πρόχειρα ταῦτα λέγουσιν, ὅτι Τὰ μετέωρα καὶ τὰ ὑπὸ
γῆς, καὶ Θεοὺς μὴ νομίζειν, καὶ Τὸν ἥττω λόγον 15
κρείττω ποιεῖν. τὰ γὰρ ἀληθῆ, οἶμαι, οὐκ ἂν

ἐθέλοιεν λέγειν, ὅτι κατάδηλοι γίγνονται προσποιού-
μενοι μὲν εἰδέναι, εἰδότες δὲ οὐδέν. ἅτε οὖν, οἶμαι,
Ε φιλότιμοι ὄντες καὶ σφοδροὶ καὶ πολλοί, καὶ ξυντεταγμένως καὶ πιθανῶς λέγοντες περὶ ἐμοῦ, ἐμπεπλήκασιν 20
ὑμῶν τὰ ὦτα καὶ πάλαι καὶ νῦν σφοδρῶς διαβάλλοντες.
ἐκ τούτων καὶ Μέλητός μοι ἐπέθετο καὶ Ἄνυτος καὶ
Λύκων, Μέλητος μὲν ὑπὲρ τῶν ποιητῶν ἀχθόμενος,
24 Ἄνυτος δὲ | ὑπὲρ τῶν δημιουργῶν καὶ τῶν πολιτικῶν,
Λύκων δὲ ὑπὲρ τῶν ῥητόρων· ὥστε, ὅπερ ἀρχόμενος 25
ἐγὼ ἔλεγον, θαυμάζοιμ᾽ ἂν εἰ οἷός τ᾽ εἴην ἐγὼ ὑμῶν
ταύτην τὴν διαβολὴν ἐξελέσθαι ἐν οὕτως ὀλίγῳ χρόνῳ
οὕτω πολλὴν γεγονυῖαν. ταῦτ᾽ ἔστιν ὑμῖν, ὦ ἄνδρες
Ἀθηναῖοι, τἀληθῆ, καὶ ὑμᾶς οὔτε μέγα οὔτε μικρὸν
ἀποκρυψάμενος ἐγὼ λέγω οὐδ᾽ ὑποστειλάμενος· καί 30
τοι οἶδα σχεδὸν ὅτι τοῖς αὐτοῖς ἀπεχθάνομαι· ὃ καὶ
τεκμήριον ὅτι ἀληθῆ λέγω καὶ ὅτι αὕτη ἐστὶν ἡ
Β διαβολὴ ἡ ἐμὴ καὶ τὰ αἴτια ταῦτά ἐστιν. καὶ ἐάν τε νῦν
ἐάν τε αὖθις ζητήσητε ταῦτα, οὕτως εὑρήσετε.

SOCRATES DEFENDS HIMSELF AGAINST
THE INDICTMENT OF MELETUS: XI–XV

XI. Περὶ μὲν οὖν ὧν οἱ πρῶτοί μου κατήγοροι
κατηγόρουν αὕτη ἐστὶν ἱκανὴ ἀπολογία πρὸς ὑμᾶς·
πρὸς δὲ Μέλητον τὸν ἀγαθόν τε καὶ φιλόπολιν, ὥς
φησι, καὶ τοὺς ὑστέρους μετὰ ταῦτα πειράσομαι
ἀπολογεῖσθαι. αὖθις γὰρ δή, ὥσπερ ἑτέρων τούτων 5
ὄντων κατηγόρων, λάβωμεν αὖ τὴν τούτων ἀντωμοσίαν. ἔχει δέ πως ὧδε· "Σωκράτη" φησὶν "ἀδικεῖν
τούς τε νέους διαφθείροντα καὶ θεοὺς οὓς ἡ πόλις

c νομίζει οὐ νομίζοντα, ἕτερα δὲ δαιμόνια καινά." τὸ μὲν
δὴ ἔγκλημα τοιοῦτόν ἐστιν· τούτου δὲ τοῦ ἐγκλήματος 10
ἐν ἕκαστον ἐξετάσωμεν. φησὶ γὰρ δὴ τοὺς νέους
ἀδικεῖν με διαφθείροντα. ἐγὼ δέ γε, ὦ ἄνδρες Ἀθηναῖοι, ἀδικεῖν φημι Μέλητον, ὅτι σπουδῇ χαριεντίζεται, ῥᾳδίως εἰς ἀγῶνας καθιστὰς ἀνθρώπους, περὶ
πραγμάτων προσποιούμενος σπουδάζειν καὶ κήδεσθαι, 15
ὧν οὐδὲν τούτῳ πώποτε ἐμέλησεν. ὡς δὲ τοῦτο
οὕτως ἔχει, πειράσομαι καὶ ὑμῖν ἐπιδεῖξαι.

XII. Καί μοι δεῦρο, ὦ Μέλητε, εἰπέ· ἄλλο τι ἢ
D περὶ πολλοῦ ποιεῖ, ὅπως ὡς βέλτιστοι οἱ νεώτεροι
ἔσονται; Ἔγωγε. Ἴθι δὴ νῦν εἰπὲ τούτοις, τίς αὐτοὺς
βελτίους ποιεῖ; δῆλον γὰρ ὅτι οἶσθα, μέλον γέ σοι.
τὸν μὲν γὰρ διαφθείροντα ἐξευρὼν ὡς φὴς ἐμὲ εἰσάγεις 5
τουτοισὶ καὶ κατηγορεῖς· τὸν δὲ δὴ βελτίους ποιοῦντα
ἴθι εἰπὲ καὶ μήνυσον αὐτοῖς, τίς ἐστιν. ὁρᾷς, ὦ
Μέλητε, ὅτι σιγᾷς καὶ οὐκ ἔχεις εἰπεῖν; καί τοι οὐκ
αἰσχρόν σοι δοκεῖ εἶναι καὶ ἱκανὸν τεκμήριον οὗ δὴ
ἐγὼ λέγω, ὅτι σοι οὐδὲν μεμέληκεν; ἀλλ' εἰπέ, ὠγαθέ, 10
E τίς αὐτοὺς ἀμείνους ποιεῖ; Οἱ νόμοι. Ἀλλ' οὐ τοῦτο
ἐρωτῶ, ὦ βέλτιστε, ἀλλὰ τίς ἄνθρωπος, ὅστις πρῶτον
καὶ αὐτὸ τοῦτο οἶδε, τοὺς νόμους. Οὗτοι, ὦ Σώκρατες,
οἱ δικασταί. Πῶς λέγεις, ὦ Μέλητε; οἴδε τοὺς νέους
παιδεύειν οἷοί τέ εἰσι καὶ βελτίους ποιοῦσιν; Μάλιστα. 15
Πότερον ἅπαντες, ἢ οἱ μὲν αὐτῶν, οἱ δ' οὔ; Ἅπαντες.
Εὖ γε νὴ τὴν Ἥραν λέγεις, καὶ πολλὴν ἀφθονίαν τῶν
ὠφελούντων. τί δὲ δή; οἴδε οἱ ἀκροαταὶ βελτίους
25 ποιοῦσιν, | ἢ οὔ; Καὶ οὗτοι. Τί δὲ οἱ βουλευταί; Καὶ
οἱ βουλευταί. Ἀλλ' ἄρα, ὦ Μέλητε, μὴ οἱ ἐν τῇ ἐκ- 20
κλησίᾳ, οἱ ἐκκλησιασταί, διαφθείρουσι τοὺς νεωτέρους;

ἢ κἀκεῖνοι βελτίους ποιοῦσιν ἅπαντες; Κἀκεῖνοι.
Πάντες ἄρα, ὡς ἔοικεν, Ἀθηναῖοι καλοὺς κἀγαθοὺς
ποιοῦσι πλὴν ἐμοῦ, ἐγὼ δὲ μόνος διαφθείρω. οὕτω
λέγεις; Πάνυ σφόδρα ταῦτα λέγω. Πολλήν γέ μου 25
κατέγνωκας δυστυχίαν. καί μοι ἀπόκριναι· ἦ καὶ περὶ
B ἵππους οὕτω σοι δοκεῖ ἔχειν· οἱ μὲν βελτίους ποιοῦντες
αὐτοὺς πάντες ἄνθρωποι εἶναι, εἷς δέ τις ὁ διαφθείρων;
ἤ, τοὐναντίον τούτου πᾶν, εἷς μέν τις ὁ βελτίους οἷός
τ' ὢν ποιεῖν ἢ πάνυ ὀλίγοι, οἱ ἱππικοί, οἱ δὲ πολλοί, 30
ἐάνπερ ξυνῶσι καὶ χρῶνται ἵπποις, διαφθείρουσιν; οὐχ
οὕτως ἔχει, ὦ Μέλητε, καὶ περὶ ἵππων καὶ τῶν ἄλλων
ἁπάντων ζῴων; πάντως δήπου, ἐάν τε σὺ καὶ Ἄνυτος
οὐ φῆτε ἐάν τε φῆτε· πολλὴ γὰρ ἄν τις εὐδαιμονία εἴη
περὶ τοὺς νέους, εἰ εἷς μὲν μόνος αὐτοὺς διαφθείρει, οἱ 35
C δ' ἄλλοι ὠφελοῦσιν. ἀλλὰ γάρ, ὦ Μέλητε, ἱκανῶς
ἐπιδείκνυσαι ὅτι οὐδεπώποτε ἐφρόντισας τῶν νέων, καὶ
σαφῶς ἀποφαίνεις τὴν σαυτοῦ ἀμέλειαν, ὅτι οὐδέν σοι
μεμέληκεν περὶ ὧν ἐμὲ εἰσάγεις.

XIII. Ἔτι δὲ ἡμῖν εἰπέ, ὦ πρὸς Διὸς Μέλητε,
πότερον ἔστιν οἰκεῖν ἄμεινον ἐν πολίταις χρηστοῖς ἢ
πονηροῖς; ὦ τάν, ἀπόκριναι· οὐδὲν γάρ τοι χαλεπὸν
ἐρωτῶ. οὐχ οἱ μὲν πονηροὶ κακόν τι ἐργάζονται τοὺς
ἀεὶ ἐγγυτάτω ἑαυτῶν ὄντας, οἱ δ' ἀγαθοὶ ἀγαθόν τι; 5
D Πάνυ γε. Ἔστιν οὖν ὅστις βούλεται ὑπὸ τῶν ξυνόντων
βλάπτεσθαι μᾶλλον ἢ ὠφελεῖσθαι; ἀποκρίνου, ὦ ἀγαθέ·
καὶ γὰρ ὁ νόμος κελεύει ἀποκρίνεσθαι. ἔσθ' ὅστις
βούλεται βλάπτεσθαι; Οὐ δῆτα. Φέρε δή, πότερον ἐμὲ
εἰσάγεις δεῦρο ὡς διαφθείροντα τοὺς νεωτέρους 10
καὶ πονηροτέρους ποιοῦντα ἑκόντα ἢ ἄκοντα; Ἑκόντα
ἔγωγε. Τί δῆτα, ὦ Μέλητε; τοσοῦτον σὺ ἐμοῦ

σοφώτερος εἶ τηλικούτου ὄντος τηλικόσδε ὤν, ὥστε
σὺ μὲν ἔγνωκας ὅτι οἱ μὲν κακοὶ κακόν τι ἐργάζονται
E ἀεὶ τοὺς μάλιστα πλησίον ἑαυτῶν, οἱ δὲ ἀγαθοὶ 15
ἀγαθόν, ἐγὼ δὲ δὴ εἰς τοσοῦτον ἀμαθίας ἥκω, ὥστε
καὶ τοῦτ' ἀγνοῶ, ὅτι, ἐάν τινα μοχθηρὸν ποιήσω τῶν
ξυνόντων, κινδυνεύσω κακόν τι λαβεῖν ὑπ' αὐτοῦ, ὥστε
τοῦτο τὸ τοσοῦτον κακὸν ἑκὼν ποιῶ, ὡς φῂς σύ; ταῦτα
ἐγώ σοι οὐ πείθομαι, ὦ Μέλητε, οἶμαι δὲ οὐδὲ ἄλλον 20
ἀνθρώπων οὐδένα· ἀλλ' ἢ οὐ διαφθείρω, ἢ εἰ δια-
26 φθείρω, | ἄκων, ὥστε σύ γε κατ' ἀμφότερα ψεύδει.

εἰ δὲ ἄκων διαφθείρω, τῶν τοιούτων καὶ ἀκουσίων
ἁμαρτημάτων οὐ δεῦρο νόμος εἰσάγειν ἐστίν, ἀλλ' ἰδίᾳ
λαβόντα διδάσκειν καὶ νουθετεῖν· δῆλον γὰρ ὅτι, ἐὰν 25
μάθω, παύσομαι ὅ γε ἄκων ποιῶ. σὺ δὲ ξυγγενέσθαι
μέν μοι καὶ διδάξαι ἔφυγες καὶ οὐκ ἠθέλησας, δεῦρο
δὲ εἰσάγεις, οἷ νόμος ἐστὶν εἰσάγειν τοὺς κολάσεως
δεομένους, ἀλλ' οὐ μαθήσεως.

XIV. Ἀλλὰ γάρ, ὦ ἄνδρες Ἀθηναῖοι, τοῦτο μὲν
B δῆλον ἤδη ἐστίν, ὃ ἐγὼ ἔλεγον, ὅτι Μελήτῳ τούτων
οὔτε μέγα οὔτε μικρὸν πώποτε ἐμέλησεν· ὅμως δὲ δὴ
λέγε ἡμῖν, πῶς με φῂς διαφθείρειν, ὦ Μέλητε, τοὺς
νεωτέρους; ἢ δῆλον δὴ ὅτι, κατὰ τὴν γραφὴν ἣν 5
ἔγραψω, θεοὺς διδάσκοντα μὴ νομίζειν οὓς ἡ πόλις
νομίζει, ἕτερα δὲ δαιμόνια καινά; οὐ ταῦτα λέγεις ὅτι
διδάσκων διαφθείρω; Πάνυ μὲν οὖν σφόδρα ταῦτα
λέγω. Πρὸς αὐτῶν τοίνυν, ὦ Μέλητε, τούτων τῶν
θεῶν, ὧν νῦν ὁ λόγος ἐστίν, εἰπὲ ἔτι σαφέστερον καὶ 10
C ἐμοὶ καὶ τοῖς ἀνδράσιν τούτοις. ἐγὼ γὰρ οὐ δύναμαι
μαθεῖν, πότερον λέγεις διδάσκειν με νομίζειν εἶναι
τινὰς θεούς, καὶ αὐτὸς ἄρα νομίζω εἶναι θεοὺς καὶ οὐκ

εἰμὶ τὸ παράπαν ἄθεος οὐδὲ ταύτῃ ἀδικῶ, οὐ μέντοι
οὕσπερ γε ἡ πόλις, ἀλλ' ἑτέρους, καὶ τοῦτ' ἔστιν ὃ 15
μοι ἐγκαλεῖς, ὅτι ἑτέρους· ἢ παντάπασί με φῂς οὔτε
αὐτὸν νομίζειν θεοὺς τούς τε ἄλλους ταῦτα διδάσκειν.
Ταῦτα λέγω, ὡς τὸ παράπαν οὐ νομίζεις θεούς. Ὦ
D θαυμάσιε Μέλητε, ἵνα τί ταῦτα λέγεις; οὐδὲ ἥλιον
οὐδὲ σελήνην ἄρα νομίζω θεοὺς εἶναι, ὥσπερ οἱ ἄλλοι 20
ἄνθρωποι; Μὰ Δί', ὦ ἄνδρες δικασταί, ἐπεὶ τὸν μὲν
ἥλιον λίθον φησὶν εἶναι, τὴν δὲ σελήνην γῆν. Ἀναξαγόρου οἴει κατηγορεῖν, ὦ φίλε Μέλητε, καὶ οὕτω
καταφρονεῖς τῶνδε καὶ οἴει αὐτοὺς ἀπείρους γραμ-
μάτων εἶναι, ὥστε οὐκ εἰδέναι ὅτι τὰ Ἀναξαγόρου 25
βιβλία τοῦ Κλαζομενίου γέμει τούτων τῶν λόγων; καὶ
δὴ καὶ οἱ νέοι ταῦτα παρ' ἐμοῦ μανθάνουσιν, ἃ ἔξεστιν
E ἐνίοτε, εἰ πάνυ πολλοῦ, δραχμῆς ἐκ τῆς ὀρχήστρας
πριαμένοις Σωκράτους καταγελᾶν, ἐὰν προσποιῆται
ἑαυτοῦ εἶναι, ἄλλως τε καὶ οὕτως ἄτοπα ὄντα. ἀλλ' 30
ὦ πρὸς Διός, οὑτωσί σοι δοκῶ; οὐδένα νομίζω θεὸν
εἶναι; Οὐ μέντοι μὰ Δί' οὐδ' ὁπωστιοῦν. Ἄπιστός γ' εἶ,
ὦ Μέλητε, καὶ ταῦτα μέντοι, ὡς ἐμοὶ δοκεῖς, σαυτῷ.
ἐμοὶ γὰρ δοκεῖ οὑτοσί, ὦ ἄνδρες Ἀθηναῖοι, πάνυ εἶναι
ὑβριστὴς καὶ ἀκόλαστος, καὶ ἀτεχνῶς τὴν γραφὴν ταύτην 35
ὕβρει τινὶ καὶ ἀκολασίᾳ καὶ νεότητι γράψασθαι. ἔοικεν
27 γὰρ ὥσπερ | αἴνιγμα ξυντιθέντι διαπειρωμένῳ, Ἆρα
γνώσεται Σωκράτης ὁ σοφὸς δὴ ἐμοῦ χαριεντιζομένου
καὶ ἐναντί' ἐμαυτῷ λέγοντος, ἢ ἐξαπατήσω αὐτὸν καὶ
τοὺς ἄλλους τοὺς ἀκούοντας; οὗτος γὰρ ἐμοὶ φαίνεται 40
τὰ ἐναντία λέγειν αὐτὸς ἑαυτῷ ἐν τῇ γραφῇ, ὥσπερ ἂν
εἰ εἴποι· Ἀδικεῖ Σωκράτης θεοὺς οὐ νομίζων, ἀλλὰ
θεοὺς νομίζων. καί τοι τοῦτό ἐστι παίζοντος.

XV. Ξυνεπισκέψασθε δή, ὦ ἄνδρες, ᾗ μοι φαίνεται
ταῦτα λέγειν· σὺ δὲ ἡμῖν ἀπόκριναι, ὦ Μέλητε· ὑμεῖς
B δέ, ὅπερ κατ' ἀρχὰς ὑμᾶς παρῃτησάμην, μέμνησθέ μοι
μὴ θορυβεῖν, ἐὰν ἐν τῷ εἰωθότι τρόπῳ τοὺς λόγους
ποιῶμαι. Ἔστιν ὅστις ἀνθρώπων, ὦ Μέλητε, ἀνθρώπεια 5
μὲν νομίζει πράγματ' εἶναι, ἀνθρώπους δὲ οὐ νομίζει;
ἀποκρινέσθω, ὦ ἄνδρες, καὶ μὴ ἄλλα καὶ ἄλλα θορυ-
βείτω· ἔσθ' ὅστις ἵππους μὲν οὐ νομίζει, ἱππικὰ δὲ
πράγματα; ἢ αὐλητὰς μὲν οὐ νομίζει εἶναι, αὐλητικὰ δὲ
πράγματα; οὐκ ἔστιν, ὦ ἄριστε ἀνδρῶν· εἰ μὴ σὺ 10
βούλει ἀποκρίνεσθαι, ἐγώ σοι λέγω καὶ τοῖς ἄλλοις
C τουτοισί. ἀλλὰ τὸ ἐπὶ τούτῳ γε ἀπόκριναι· ἔσθ' ὅστις
δαιμόνια μὲν νομίζει πράγματ' εἶναι, δαίμονας δὲ οὐ
νομίζει; Οὐκ ἔστιν. Ὡς ὤνησας, ὅτι μόγις ἀπεκρίνω
ὑπὸ τουτωνὶ ἀναγκαζόμενος. οὐκοῦν δαιμόνια μὲν φῄς 15
με καὶ νομίζειν καὶ διδάσκειν· εἴτ' οὖν καινὰ εἴτε
παλαιά, ἀλλ' οὖν δαιμόνιά γε νομίζω κατὰ τὸν σὸν
λόγον, καὶ ταῦτα καὶ διωμόσω ἐν τῇ ἀντιγραφῇ. εἰ δὲ
δαιμόνια νομίζω, καὶ δαίμονας δήπου πολλὴ ἀνάγκη
νομίζειν μέ ἐστιν· οὐχ οὕτως ἔχει; ἔχει δή· τίθημι γάρ 20
D σε ὁμολογοῦντα, ἐπειδὴ οὐκ ἀποκρίνει. τοὺς δὲ
δαίμονας οὐχὶ ἤτοι θεούς γε ἡγούμεθα ἢ θεῶν παῖδας;
φῂς ἢ οὔ; Πάνυ γε. Οὐκοῦν εἴπερ δαίμονας ἡγοῦμαι,
ὡς σὺ φῄς, εἰ μὲν θεοί τινές εἰσιν οἱ δαίμονες, τοῦτ' ἂν
εἴη ὃ ἐγώ φημί σε αἰνίττεσθαι καὶ χαριεντίζεσθαι, 25
θεοὺς οὐχ ἡγούμενον φάναι ἐμὲ θεοὺς αὖ ἡγεῖσθαι
πάλιν, ἐπειδήπερ γε δαίμονας ἡγοῦμαι· εἰ δ' αὖ οἱ
δαίμονες θεῶν παῖδές εἰσι νόθοι τινὲς ἢ ἐκ νυμφῶν ἢ ἔκ
τινων ἄλλων, ὧν δὴ καὶ λέγονται, τίς ἂν ἀνθρώπων
E θεῶν μὲν παῖδας ἡγοῖτο εἶναι, θεοὺς δὲ μή; ὁμοίως 30

35

γὰρ ἂν ἄτοπον εἴη, ὥσπερ ἂν εἴ τις ἵππων μὲν παῖδας
ἡγοῖτο ἢ καὶ ὄνων [τοὺς ἡμιόνους,] ἵππους δὲ καὶ
ὄνους μὴ ἡγοῖτο εἶναι. ἀλλ᾿, ὦ Μέλητε, οὐκ ἔστιν ὅπως
σὺ ταῦτα οὐχὶ ἀποπειρώμενος ἡμῶν ἐγράψω τὴν γραφὴν
ταύτην, ἢ ἀπορῶν ὅ τι ἐγκαλοῖς ἐμοὶ ἀληθὲς ἀδίκημα· 35
ὅπως δὲ σύ τινα πείθοις ἂν καὶ σμικρὸν νοῦν ἔχοντα
ἀνθρώπων, ὡς οὐ τοῦ αὐτοῦ ἐστιν καὶ δαιμόνια καὶ
θεῖα ⟨καὶ δαίμονας καὶ θεοὺς⟩ ἡγεῖσθαι, καὶ αὖ τοῦ
αὐτοῦ ⟨μήτε δαιμόνια μήτε θεῖα⟩ μήτε δαίμονας μήτε
28 θεοὺς [μήτε | ἥρωας,] οὐδεμία μηχανή ἐστιν.   40

SOCRATES DEFENDS HIS VOCATION AGAINST
POPULAR REPROACHES: XVI–XXII

(a) that through it his life is in danger (XVI–XVIII).

(b) that he holds aloof from politics (XIX–XX).

(c) that his pupils have proved dangerous to the com-
monwealth (XXI–XXII).

XVI. Ἀλλὰ γάρ, ὦ ἄνδρες Ἀθηναῖοι, ὡς μὲν ἐγὼ
οὐκ ἀδικῶ κατὰ τὴν Μελήτου γραφήν, οὐ πολλῆς μοι
δοκεῖ εἶναι ἀπολογίας, ἀλλὰ ἱκανὰ καὶ ταῦτα· ὃ δὲ καὶ
ἐν τοῖς ἔμπροσθεν ἔλεγον, ὅτι πολλή μοι ἀπέχθεια
γέγονεν καὶ πρὸς πολλούς, εὖ ἴστε ὅτι ἀληθές ἐστιν. 5
καὶ τοῦτ᾿ ἔστιν ὃ ἐμὲ αἱρήσει, ἐάνπερ αἱρῇ, οὐ Μέλητος
οὐδὲ Ἄνυτος, ἀλλ᾿ ἡ τῶν πολλῶν διαβολή τε καὶ
φθόνος. ἃ δὴ πολλοὺς καὶ ἄλλους καὶ ἀγαθοὺς ἄνδρας
B ᾕρηκεν, οἶμαι δὲ καὶ αἱρήσειν· οὐδὲν δὲ δεινὸν μὴ ἐν
ἐμοὶ στῇ. ἴσως δ᾿ ἂν οὖν εἴποι τις· Εἶτ᾿ οὐκ αἰσχύνει 10
ὦ Σώκρατες, τοιοῦτον ἐπιτήδευμα ἐπιτηδεύσας, ἐξ οὗ
κινδυνεύεις νυνὶ ἀποθανεῖν; ἐγὼ δὲ τούτῳ ἂν δίκαιον

λόγον ἀντείποιμι, ὅτι οὐ καλῶς λέγεις, ὦ ἄνθρωπε, εἰ
οἴει δεῖν κίνδυνον ὑπολογίζεσθαι τοῦ ζῆν ἢ τεθνάναι
ἄνδρα ὅτου τι καὶ σμικρὸν ὄφελός ἐστιν, ἀλλ᾽ οὐκ 15
ἐκεῖνο μόνον σκοπεῖν, ὅταν πράττῃ, πότερον δίκαια ἢ
ἄδικα πράττει, καὶ ἀνδρὸς ἀγαθοῦ ἔργα ἢ κακοῦ.
c φαῦλοι γὰρ ἂν τῷ γε σῷ λόγῳ εἶεν τῶν ἡμιθέων ὅσοι ἐν
Τροίᾳ τετελευτήκασιν οἵ τε ἄλλοι καὶ ὁ τῆς Θέτιδος
υἱός, ὃς τοσοῦτον τοῦ κινδύνου κατεφρόνησεν παρὰ τὸ 20
αἰσχρόν τι ὑπομεῖναι, ὥστε ἐπειδὴ εἶπεν ἡ μήτηρ
αὐτῷ προθυμουμένῳ Ἕκτορα ἀποκτεῖναι, θεὸς οὖσα,
οὑτωσί πως, ὡς ἐγὼ οἶμαι· Ὦ παῖ, εἰ τιμωρήσεις Πα-
τρόκλῳ τῷ ἑταίρῳ τὸν φόνον καὶ Ἕκτορα ἀποκτενεῖς,
αὐτὸς ἀποθανεῖ· "αὐτίκα γάρ τοι," φησί, "μεθ᾽ 25
Ἕκτορα πότμος ἑτοῖμος". ὁ δὲ ταῦτα ἀκούσας τοῦ
μὲν θανάτου καὶ τοῦ κινδύνου ὠλιγώρησε, πολὺ δὲ
d μᾶλλον δείσας τὸ ζῆν κακὸς ὢν καὶ τοῖς φίλοις μὴ
τιμωρεῖν, "Αὐτίκα", φησί, "τεθναίην" δίκην ἐπιθεὶς
τῷ ἀδικοῦντι, ἵνα μὴ ἐνθάδε μένω καταγέλαστος "παρὰ 30
νηυσὶ κορωνίσιν ἄχθος ἀρούρης". μὴ αὐτὸν οἴει
φροντίσαι θανάτου καὶ κινδύνου; οὕτω γὰρ ἔχει, ὦ
ἄνδρες Ἀθηναῖοι, τῇ ἀληθείᾳ· οὗ ἄν τις ἑαυτὸν τάξῃ
ἡγησάμενος βέλτιστον εἶναι ἢ ὑπ᾽ ἄρχοντος ταχθῇ,
ἐνταῦθα δεῖ, ὡς ἐμοὶ δοκεῖ, μένοντα κινδυνεύειν, 35
μηδὲν ὑπολογιζόμενον μήτε θάνατον μήτε ἄλλο μηδὲν
πρὸ τοῦ αἰσχροῦ.

XVII. Ἐγὼ οὖν δεινὰ ἂν εἴην εἰργασμένος, ὦ
e ἄνδρες Ἀθηναῖοι, εἰ, ὅτε μέν με οἱ ἄρχοντες ἔταττον,
οὓς ὑμεῖς εἵλεσθε ἄρχειν μου, καὶ ἐν Ποτειδαίᾳ καὶ
ἐν Ἀμφιπόλει καὶ ἐπὶ Δηλίῳ, τότε μὲν οὗ ἐκεῖνοι
ἔταττον ἔμενον ὥσπερ καὶ ἄλλος τις καὶ ἐκινδύνευον 5

ἀποθανεῖν, τοῦ δὲ θεοῦ τάττοντος, ὡς ἐγὼ ᾠήθην τε
καὶ ὑπέλαβον, φιλοσοφοῦντά με δεῖν ζῆν καὶ ἐξετάζοντα ἐμαυτὸν καὶ τοὺς ἄλλους, ἐνταῦθα δὲ φοβηθεὶς
29 ἢ θάνατον ἢ ἄλλο | ὁτιοῦν πρᾶγμα λίποιμι τὴν τάξιν.
δεινὸν τἂν εἴη, καὶ ὡς ἀληθῶς τότ' ἄν με δικαίως 10
εἰσάγοι τις εἰς δικαστήριον, ὅτι οὐ νομίζω θεοὺς εἶναι
ἀπειθῶν τῇ μαντείᾳ καὶ δεδιὼς θάνατον καὶ οἰόμενος
σοφὸς εἶναι οὐκ ὤν. τὸ γάρ τοι θάνατον δεδιέναι, ὦ
ἄνδρες, οὐδὲν ἄλλο ἐστὶν ἢ δοκεῖν σοφὸν εἶναι μὴ ὄντα ·
δοκεῖν γὰρ εἰδέναι ἐστὶν ἃ οὐκ οἶδεν. οἶδε μὲν γὰρ 15
οὐδεὶς τὸν θάνατον οὐδ' εἰ τυγχάνει τῷ ἀνθρώπῳ
πάντων μέγιστον ὂν τῶν ἀγαθῶν, δεδίασι δ' ὡς εὖ
B εἰδότες ὅτι μέγιστον τῶν κακῶν ἐστί. καὶ τοῦτο πῶς
οὐκ ἀμαθία ἐστὶν αὕτη ἡ ἐπονείδιστος, ἡ τοῦ οἴεσθαι
εἰδέναι ἃ οὐκ οἶδεν; ἐγὼ δ', ὦ ἄνδρες, τούτῳ καὶ 20
ἐνταῦθα ἴσως διαφέρω τῶν πολλῶν ἀνθρώπων, καὶ εἰ
δή τῳ σοφώτερός του φαίην εἶναι, τούτῳ ἄν, ὅτι οὐκ
εἰδὼς ἱκανῶς περὶ τῶν ἐν Ἅιδου οὕτω καὶ οἴομαι οὐκ
εἰδέναι · τὸ δὲ ἀδικεῖν καὶ ἀπειθεῖν τῷ βελτίονι, καὶ
θεῷ καὶ ἀνθρώπῳ, ὅτι κακὸν καὶ αἰσχρόν ἐστιν οἶδα. 25
πρὸ οὖν τῶν κακῶν, ὧν οἶδα ὅτι κακά ἐστιν, ἃ μὴ οἶδα
εἰ ἀγαθὰ ὄντα τυγχάνει, οὐδέποτε φοβήσομαι οὐδὲ
C φεύξομαι · ὥστε οὐδ' εἴ με νῦν ὑμεῖς ἀφίετε Ἀνύτῳ
ἀπιστήσαντες, ὃς ἔφη ἢ τὴν ἀρχὴν οὐ δεῖν ἐμὲ δεῦρο
εἰσελθεῖν ἤ, ἐπειδὴ εἰσῆλθον, οὐχ οἷόν τ' εἶναι τὸ μὴ 30
ἀποκτεῖναί με, λέγων πρὸς ὑμᾶς ὡς, εἰ διαφευξοίμην,
ἤδη ἂν ὑμῶν οἱ υἱεῖς ἐπιτηδεύοντες ἃ Σωκράτης
διδάσκει πάντες παντάπασι διαφθαρήσονται,—εἴ μοι
πρὸς ταῦτα εἴποιτε · Ὦ Σώκρατες, νῦν μὲν Ἀνύτῳ οὐ
πεισόμεθα, ἀλλ' ἀφίεμέν σε, ἐπὶ τούτῳ μέντοι, ἐφ' 35

ὦτε μηκέτι ἐν ταύτῃ τῇ ζητήσει διατρίβειν μηδὲ
D φιλοσοφεῖν· ἐὰν δὲ ἁλῷ ἔτι τοῦτο πράττων, ἀποθανεῖ·
εἰ οὖν με, ὅπερ εἶπον, ἐπὶ τούτοις ἀφίοιτε, εἴποιμ' ἂν
ὑμῖν ὅτι Ἐγὼ ὑμᾶς, ἄνδρες Ἀθηναῖοι, ἀσπάζομαι μὲν
καὶ φιλῶ, πείσομαι δὲ μᾶλλον τῷ θεῷ ἢ ὑμῖν, καὶ 40
ἔωσπερ ἂν ἐμπνέω καὶ οἷός τε ὦ, οὐ μὴ παύσωμαι
φιλοσοφῶν καὶ ὑμῖν παρακελευόμενός τε καὶ ἐνδεικ-
νύμενος ὅτῳ ἂν ἀεὶ ἐντυγχάνω ὑμῶν, λέγων οἷάπερ
εἴωθα, ὅτι Ὦ ἄριστε ἀνδρῶν, Ἀθηναῖος ὤν, πόλεως
τῆς μεγίστης καὶ εὐδοκιμωτάτης εἰς σοφίαν καὶ 45
ἰσχύν, χρημάτων μὲν οὐκ αἰσχύνει ἐπιμελούμενος,
E ὅπως σοι ἔσται ὡς πλεῖστα, καὶ δόξης καὶ τιμῆς,
φρονήσεως δὲ καὶ ἀληθείας καὶ τῆς ψυχῆς, ὅπως ὡς
βελτίστη ἔσται, οὐκ ἐπιμελεῖ οὐδὲ φροντίζεις; καὶ
ἐάν τις ὑμῶν ἀμφισβητῇ καὶ φῇ ἐπιμελεῖσθαι, οὐκ 50
εὐθὺς ἀφήσω αὐτὸν οὐδ' ἄπειμι, ἀλλ' ἐρήσομαι αὐτὸν
καὶ ἐξετάσω καὶ ἐλέγξω, καὶ ἐάν μοι μὴ δοκῇ κεκτῆ-
σθαι ἀρετήν, φάναι δέ, ὀνειδιῶ ὅτι τὰ πλείστου ἄξια
30 περὶ | ἐλαχίστου ποιεῖται, τὰ δὲ φαυλότερα περὶ
πλείονος. ταῦτα καὶ νεωτέρῳ καὶ πρεσβυτέρῳ, ὅτῳ 55
ἂν ἐντυγχάνω, ποιήσω, καὶ ξένῳ καὶ ἀστῷ, μᾶλλον δὲ
τοῖς ἀστοῖς, ὅσῳ μου ἐγγυτέρω ἐστὲ γένει. ταῦτα γὰρ
κελεύει ὁ θεός, εὖ ἴστε, καὶ ἐγὼ οἶμαι οὐδέν πω ὑμῖν
μεῖζον ἀγαθὸν γενέσθαι ἐν τῇ πόλει ἢ τὴν ἐμὴν τῷ
θεῷ ὑπηρεσίαν. οὐδὲν γὰρ ἄλλο πράττων ἐγὼ περι- 60
έρχομαι ἢ πείθων ὑμῶν καὶ νεωτέρους καὶ πρεσβυτέρους
B μήτε σωμάτων ἐπιμελεῖσθαι μήτε χρημάτων πρότερον
μηδὲ οὕτω σφόδρα ὡς τῆς ψυχῆς, ὅπως ὡς ἀρίστη
ἔσται, λέγων· Οὐκ ἐκ χρημάτων ἀρετὴ γίγνεται, ἀλλ'
ἐξ ἀρετῆς χρήματα καὶ τὰ ἄλλα ἀγαθὰ τοῖς ἀνθρώποις 65

39

ἅπαντα καὶ ἰδίᾳ καὶ δημοσίᾳ. εἰ μὲν οὖν ταῦτα λέγων
διαφθείρω τοὺς νέους, ταῦτ᾽ ἂν εἴη βλαβερά· εἰ δέ τίς
μέ φησιν ἄλλα λέγειν ἢ ταῦτα, οὐδὲν λέγει. πρὸς
ταῦτα, φαίην ἄν, ὦ ᾽Αθηναῖοι, ἢ πείθεσθε ᾽Ανύτῳ ἢ
μή, καὶ ἢ ἀφίετε ἢ μὴ ἀφίετε, ὡς ἐμοῦ οὐκ ἂν ποιή- 70
C σοντος ἄλλα, οὐδ᾽ εἰ μέλλω πολλάκις τεθνάναι.

XVIII. Μὴ θορυβεῖτε, ἄνδρες ᾽Αθηναῖοι, ἀλλ᾽
ἐμμείνατέ μοι οἷς ἐδεήθην ὑμῶν, μὴ θορυβεῖν ἐφ᾽ οἷς
ἂν λέγω, ἀλλ᾽ ἀκούειν· καὶ γάρ, ὡς ἐγὼ οἶμαι,
ὀνήσεσθε ἀκούοντες. μέλλω γὰρ οὖν ἄττα ὑμῖν ἐρεῖν
καὶ ἄλλα, ἐφ᾽ οἷς ἴσως βοήσεσθε· ἀλλὰ μηδαμῶς 5
ποιεῖτε τοῦτο. εὖ γὰρ ἴστε, ἐὰν ἐμὲ ἀποκτείνητε
τοιοῦτον ὄντα, οἷον ἐγὼ λέγω, οὐκ ἐμὲ μείζω βλάψετε
ἢ ὑμᾶς αὐτούς· ἐμὲ μὲν γὰρ οὐδὲν ἂν βλάψειεν οὔτε
D Μέλητος οὔτε ῎Ανυτος· οὐδὲ γὰρ ἂν δύναιτο· οὐ γὰρ
οἶμαι θεμιτὸν εἶναι ἀμείνονι ἀνδρὶ ὑπὸ χείρονος 10
βλάπτεσθαι. ἀποκτείνειε μεντἂν ἴσως ἢ ἐξελάσειεν ἢ
ἀτιμώσειεν· ἀλλὰ ταῦτα οὗτος μὲν ἴσως οἴεται καὶ
ἄλλος τίς που μεγάλα κακά, ἐγὼ δ᾽ οὐκ οἴομαι, ἀλλὰ
πολὺ μᾶλλον ποιεῖν ἃ οὗτος νυνὶ ποιεῖ, ἄνδρα ἀδίκως
ἐπιχειρεῖν ἀποκτεινύναι. νῦν οὖν, ὦ ἄνδρες ᾽Αθηναῖοι, 15
πολλοῦ δέω ἐγὼ ὑπὲρ ἐμαυτοῦ ἀπολογεῖσθαι, ὥς τις ἂν
οἴοιτο, ἀλλὰ ὑπὲρ ὑμῶν, μή τι ἐξαμάρτητε περὶ τὴν
E τοῦ θεοῦ δόσιν ὑμῖν ἐμοῦ καταψηφισάμενοι. ἐὰν γὰρ
ἐμὲ ἀποκτείνητε, οὐ ῥᾳδίως ἄλλον τοιοῦτον εὑρήσετε,
ἀτεχνῶς, εἰ καὶ γελοιότερον εἰπεῖν, προσκείμενον τῇ 20
πόλει ὑπὸ τοῦ θεοῦ, ὥσπερ ἵππῳ μεγάλῳ μὲν καὶ
γενναίῳ, ὑπὸ μεγέθους δὲ νωθεστέρῳ καὶ δεομένῳ
ἐγείρεσθαι ὑπὸ μύωπός τινος· οἷον δή δοκεῖ μοι ὁ θεὸς
ἐμὲ τῇ πόλει προστεθεικέναι τοιοῦτόν τινα, ὃς ὑμᾶς

ἐγείρων καὶ πείθων καὶ ὀνειδίζων ἕνα ἕκαστον, οὐδὲν 25
31 παύομαι | τὴν ἡμέραν ὅλην πανταχοῦ προσκαθίζων.
τοιοῦτος οὖν ἄλλος οὐ ῥᾳδίως ὑμῖν γενήσεται, ὦ
ἄνδρες, ἀλλ' ἐὰν ἐμοὶ πείθησθε, φείσεσθέ μου· ὑμεῖς
δ' ἴσως τάχ' ἂν ἀχθόμενοι, ὥσπερ οἱ νυστάζοντες
ἐγειρόμενοι, κρούσαντες ἄν με, πειθόμενοι Ἀνύτῳ, 30
ῥᾳδίως ἂν ἀποκτείναιτε, εἶτα τὸν λοιπὸν βίον καθεύ-
δοντες διατελοῖτε ἄν, εἰ μή τινα ἄλλον ὁ θεὸς ὑμῖν ἐπι-
πέμψειεν κηδόμενος ὑμῶν. ὅτι δ' ἐγὼ τυγχάνω ὢν
τοιοῦτος, οἷος ὑπὸ τοῦ θεοῦ τῇ πόλει δεδόσθαι, ἐνθένδε
B ἂν κατανοήσαιτε· οὐ γὰρ ἀνθρωπίνῳ ἔοικε τὸ ἐμὲ τῶν 35
μὲν ἐμαυτοῦ ἁπάντων ἠμεληκέναι καὶ ἀνέχεσθαι τῶν
οἰκείων ἀμελουμένων τοσαῦτα ἤδη ἔτη, τὸ δὲ ὑμέτερον
πράττειν ἀεί, ἰδίᾳ ἑκάστῳ προσιόντα ὥσπερ πατέρα ἢ
ἀδελφὸν πρεσβύτερον, πείθοντα ἐπιμελεῖσθαι ἀρετῆς.
καί τοι εἰ μέν τι ἀπὸ τούτων ἀπέλαυον καὶ μισθὸν 40
λαμβάνων ταῦτα παρεκελευόμην, εἶχον ἄν τινα λόγον·
νῦν δὲ ὁρᾶτε δὴ καὶ αὐτοί, ὅτι οἱ κατήγοροι τἆλλα
πάντα ἀναισχύντως οὕτω κατηγοροῦντες τοῦτό γε
C οὐχ οἷοί τε ἐγένοντο ἀπαναισχυντῆσαι παρασχόμενοι
μάρτυρα, ὡς ἐγώ ποτέ τινα ἢ ἐπραξάμην μισθὸν ἢ 45
ᾔτησα. ἱκανὸν γάρ, οἶμαι, ἐγὼ παρέχομαι τὸν
μάρτυρα, ὡς ἀληθῆ λέγω, τὴν πενίαν.

XIX. Ἴσως ἂν οὖν δόξειεν ἄτοπον εἶναι, ὅτι δὴ
ἐγὼ ἰδίᾳ μὲν ταῦτα ξυμβουλεύω περιιὼν καὶ πολυπραγ-
μονῶ, δημοσίᾳ δὲ οὐ τολμῶ ἀναβαίνων εἰς τὸ πλῆθος
τὸ ὑμέτερον ξυμβουλεύειν τῇ πόλει. τούτου δὲ αἴτιόν
D ἐστιν ὃ ὑμεῖς πολλάκις ἀκηκόατε πολλαχοῦ λέγοντος, 5
ὅτι μοι θεῖόν τι καὶ δαιμόνιον γίγνεται [φωνή,] ὃ δὴ
καὶ ἐν τῇ γραφῇ ἐπικωμῳδῶν Μέλητος ἐγράψατο· ἐμοὶ

δὲ τοῦτ' ἐστὶν ἐκ παιδὸς ἀρξάμενον, φωνή τις γιγνομένη, ἣ ὅταν γένηται, ἀεὶ ἀποτρέπει με τοῦτο ὃ ἂν
μέλλω πράττειν, προτρέπει δὲ οὔποτε· τοῦτ' ἔστιν ὅ 10
μοι ἐναντιοῦται τὰ πολιτικὰ πράττειν. καὶ παγκάλως
γέ μοι δοκεῖ ἐναντιοῦσθαι· εὖ γὰρ ἴστε, ὦ ἄνδρες
Ἀθηναῖοι, εἰ ἐγὼ πάλαι ἐπεχείρησα πράττειν τὰ
πολιτικὰ πράγματα, πάλαι ἂν ἀπολώλη καὶ οὔτ' ἂν
E ὑμᾶς ὠφελήκη οὐδὲν οὔτ' ἂν ἐμαυτόν. καί μοι μὴ 15
ἄχθεσθε λέγοντι τἀληθῆ· οὐ γὰρ ἔστιν ὅστις ἀνθρώπων
σωθήσεται οὔτε ὑμῖν οὔτε ἄλλῳ πλήθει οὐδενὶ γνησίως
ἐναντιούμενος καὶ διακωλύων πολλὰ ἄδικα καὶ παρά-
32 νομα ἐν τῇ πόλει γίγνεσθαι, | ἀλλ' ἀναγκαῖόν ἐστι
τὸν τῷ ὄντι μαχούμενον ὑπὲρ τοῦ δικαίου, καὶ εἰ 20
μέλλει ὀλίγον χρόνον σωθήσεσθαι, ἰδιωτεύειν ἀλλὰ μὴ
δημοσιεύειν.

XX. Μεγάλα δ' ἔγωγε ὑμῖν τεκμήρια παρέξομαι
τούτων, οὐ λόγους, ἀλλ' ὃ ὑμεῖς τιμᾶτε, ἔργα. ἀκού-
σατε δή μου τὰ ἐμοὶ ξυμβεβηκότα, ἵνα εἰδῆτε ὅτι οὐδ'
ἂν ἑνὶ ὑπεικάθοιμι παρὰ τὸ δίκαιον δείσας θάνατον, μὴ
ὑπείκων δὲ ἅμα καὶ ἅμα ἂν ἀπολοίμην. ἐρῶ δὲ ὑμῖν 5
B φορτικὰ μὲν καὶ δικανικά, ἀληθῆ δέ. ἐγὼ γάρ, ὦ
Ἀθηναῖοι, ἄλλην μὲν ἀρχὴν οὐδεμίαν πώποτε ἦρξα ἐν
τῇ πόλει, ἐβούλευσα δέ· καὶ ἔτυχεν ἡμῶν ἡ φυλὴ
Ἀντιοχὶς πρυτανεύουσα, ὅτε ὑμεῖς τοὺς δέκα στρατηγοὺς τοὺς οὐκ ἀνελομένους τοὺς ἐκ τῆς ναυμαχίας 10
ἐβούλεσθε ἀθρόους κρίνειν, παρανόμως, ὡς ἐν τῷ
ὑστέρῳ χρόνῳ πᾶσιν ὑμῖν ἔδοξε. τότ' ἐγὼ μόνος τῶν
πρυτάνεων ἠναντιώθην μηδὲν ποιεῖν παρὰ τοὺς νόμους
καὶ ἐναντία ἐψηφισάμην, καὶ ἑτοίμων ὄντων ἐνδεικνύναι με καὶ ἀπάγειν τῶν ῥητόρων, καὶ ὑμῶν κελευόντων 15

c καὶ βοώντων, μετὰ τοῦ νόμου καὶ τοῦ δικαίου ὤμην
μᾶλλόν με δεῖν διακινδυνεύειν ἢ μεθ' ὑμῶν γενέσθαι
μὴ δίκαια βουλευομένων, φοβηθέντα δεσμὸν ἢ θάνατον.
καὶ ταῦτα μὲν ἦν ἔτι δημοκρατουμένης τῆς πόλεως·
ἐπειδὴ δὲ ὀλιγαρχία ἐγένετο, οἱ τριάκοντα αὖ μετα- 20
πεμψάνεμοί με πέμπτον αὐτὸν εἰς τὴν θόλον προσέταξαν
ἀγαγεῖν ἐκ Σαλαμῖνος Λέοντα τὸν Σαλαμίνιον, ἵνα
ἀποθάνοι· οἷα δὴ καὶ ἄλλοις ἐκεῖνοι πολλοῖς πολλὰ
προσέταττον, βουλόμενοι ὡς πλείστους ἀναπλῆσαι
D αἰτιῶν· τότε μέντοι ἐγὼ οὐ λόγῳ ἀλλ' ἔργῳ αὖ 25
ἐνεδειξάμην, ὅτι ἐμοὶ θανάτου μὲν μέλει, εἰ μὴ ἀγροι-
κότερον ἦν εἰπεῖν, οὐδ' ὁτιοῦν, τοῦ δὲ μηδὲν ἄδικον
μηδ' ἀνόσιον ἐργάζεσθαι, τούτου δὲ τὸ πᾶν μέλει.
ἐμὲ γὰρ ἐκείνη ἡ ἀρχὴ οὐκ ἐξέπληξεν οὕτως ἰσχυρὰ
οὖσα, ὥστε ἄδικόν τι ἐργάσασθαι, ἀλλ' ἐπειδὴ ἐκ τῆς 30
θόλου ἐξήλθομεν, οἱ μὲν τέτταρες ᾤχοντο εἰς Σαλαμῖνα
καὶ ἤγαγον Λέοντα, ἐγὼ δὲ ᾠχόμην ἀπιὼν οἴκαδε. καὶ
ἴσως ἂν διὰ ταῦτα ἀπέθανον, εἰ μὴ ἡ ἀρχὴ διὰ ταχέων
E κατελύθη· καὶ τούτων ὑμῖν ἔσονται πολλοὶ μάρτυρες.

XXI. Ἆρ' οὖν ἂν με οἴεσθε τοσάδε ἔτη διαγε-
νέσθαι, εἰ ἔπραττον τὰ δημόσια, καὶ πράττων ἀξίως
ἀνδρὸς ἀγαθοῦ ἐβοήθουν τοῖς δικαίοις καί, ὥσπερ χρή,
τοῦτο περὶ πλείστου ἐποιούμην; πολλοῦ γε δεῖ, ὦ
ἄνδρες Ἀθηναῖοι. οὐδὲ γὰρ ἂν ἄλλος ἀνθρώπων οὐδείς. | 5
33 ἀλλ' ἐγὼ διὰ παντὸς τοῦ βίου δημοσίᾳ τε, εἴ πού
τι ἔπραξα, τοιοῦτος φανοῦμαι, καὶ ἰδίᾳ ὁ αὐτὸς οὗτος,
οὐδενὶ πώποτε ξυγχωρήσας οὐδὲν παρὰ τὸ δίκαιον
οὔτε ἄλλῳ οὔτε τούτων οὐδενί, οὓς οἱ διαβάλλοντές
ἐμέ φασιν ἐμοὺς μαθητὰς εἶναι. ἐγὼ δὲ διδάσκαλος μὲν 10
οὐδενὸς πώποτ' ἐγενόμην· εἰ δέ τίς μου λέγοντος καὶ

τὰ ἐμαυτοῦ πράττοντος ἐπιθυμεῖ ἀκούειν, εἴτε νεώτερος
εἴτε πρεσβύτερος, οὐδενὶ πώποτε ἐφθόνησα, οὐδὲ χρή-
B ματα μὲν λαμβάνων διαλέγομαι, μὴ λαμβάνων δὲ οὔ,
ἀλλ᾽ ὁμοίως καὶ πλουσίῳ καὶ πένητι παρέχω ἐμαυτὸν 15
ἐρωτᾶν, καὶ ἐάν τις βούληται ἀποκρινόμενος ἀκούειν
ὧν ἂν λέγω. καὶ τούτων ἐγὼ εἴτε τις χρηστὸς γίγνεται
εἴτε μή, οὐκ ἂν δικαίως τὴν αἰτίαν ὑπέχοιμι, ὧν μήτε
ὑπεσχόμην μηδενὶ μηδὲν πώποτε μάθημα μήτε ἐδίδαξα·
εἰ δέ τίς φησι παρ᾽ ἐμοῦ πώποτέ τι μαθεῖν ἢ ἀκοῦσαι ἰδίᾳ 20
ὅ τι μὴ καὶ ἄλλοι πάντες, εὖ ἴστε ὅτι οὐκ ἀληθῆ λέγει.

XXII. Ἀλλὰ διὰ τί δή ποτε μετ᾽ ἐμοῦ χαίρουσί
τινες πολὺν χρόνον διατρίβοντες; ἀκηκόατε, ὦ ἄνδρες
C Ἀθηναῖοι· πᾶσαν ὑμῖν τὴν ἀλήθειαν ἐγὼ εἶπον· ὅτι
ἀκούοντες χαίρουσιν ἐξεταζομένοις τοῖς οἰομένοις μὲν
εἶναι σοφοῖς, οὖσι δ᾽ οὔ· ἔστι γὰρ οὐκ ἀηδές. ἐμοὶ δὲ 5
τοῦτο, ὡς ἐγώ φημι, προστέτακται ὑπὸ τοῦ θεοῦ
πράττειν καὶ ἐκ μαντειῶν καὶ ἐξ ἐνυπνίων καὶ παντὶ
τρόπῳ, ᾧπερ τίς ποτε καὶ ἄλλη θεία μοῖρα ἀνθρώπῳ
καὶ ὁτιοῦν προσέταξε πράττειν. ταῦτα, ὦ Ἀθηναῖοι,
καὶ ἀληθῆ ἐστιν καὶ εὐέλεγκτα. εἰ γὰρ δὴ ἔγωγε τῶν 10
D νέων τοὺς μὲν διαφθείρω, τοὺς δὲ διέφθαρκα, χρῆν
δήπου, εἴτε τινὲς αὐτῶν πρεσβύτεροι γενόμενοι
ἔγνωσαν ὅτι νέοις οὖσιν αὐτοῖς ἐγὼ κακὸν πώποτέ τι
ξυνεβούλευσα, νυνὶ αὐτοὺς ἀναβαίνοντας ἐμοῦ κατηγορεῖν καὶ τιμωρεῖσθαι· εἰ δὲ μὴ αὐτοὶ ἤθελον, τῶν 15
οἰκείων τινὰς τῶν ἐκείνων, πατέρας καὶ ἀδελφοὺς καὶ
ἄλλους τοὺς προσήκοντας, εἴπερ ὑπ᾽ ἐμοῦ τι κακὸν
ἐπεπόνθεσαν αὐτῶν οἱ οἰκεῖοι, νῦν μεμνῆσθαι καὶ
τιμωρεῖσθαι. πάντως δὲ πάρεισιν αὐτῶν πολλοὶ
ἐνταυθοῖ, οὓς ἐγὼ ὁρῶ, πρῶτον μὲν Κρίτων οὑτοσί, 20

E ἐμὸς ἡλικιώτης καὶ δημότης, Κριτοβούλου τοῦδε
πατήρ· ἔπειτα Λυσανίας ὁ Σφήττιος, Αἰσχίνου τοῦδε
πατήρ· ἔτι Ἀντιφῶν ὁ Κηφισιεὺς οὑτοσί, Ἐπιγένους
πατήρ· ἄλλοι τοίνυν οὗτοι, ὧν οἱ ἀδελφοὶ ἐν ταύτῃ τῇ
διατριβῇ γεγόνασιν, Νικόστρατος Θεοζοτίδου, ἀδελφὸς 25
Θεοδότου—καὶ ὁ μὲν Θεόδοτος τετελεύτηκεν, ὥστε
οὐκ ἂν ἐκεῖνός γε αὐτοῦ καταδεηθείη—, καὶ Πάραλος
34 ὅδε, ὁ Δημοδόκου, οὗ ἦν Θεάγης ἀδελφός· ὅδε δὲ |
Ἀδείμαντος, ὁ Ἀρίστωνος, οὗ ἀδελφὸς οὑτοσὶ
Πλάτων, καὶ Αἰαντόδωρος, οὗ Ἀπολλόδωρος ὅδε 30
ἀδελφός. καὶ ἄλλους πολλοὺς ἐγὼ ἔχω ὑμῖν εἰπεῖν,
ὧν τινὰ ἐχρῆν μάλιστα μὲν ἐν τῷ ἑαυτοῦ λόγῳ παρα-
σχέσθαι Μέλητον μάρτυρα· εἰ δὲ τότε ἐπελάθετο, νῦν
παρασχέσθω, ἐγὼ παραχωρῶ, καὶ λεγέτω, εἴ τι ἔχει
τοιοῦτον. ἀλλὰ τούτου πᾶν τοὐναντίον εὑρήσετε, ὦ 35
ἄνδρες, πάντας ἐμοὶ βοηθεῖν ἑτοίμους τῷ διαφθείροντι,
τῷ κακὰ ἐργαζομένῳ τοὺς οἰκείους αὐτῶν, ὥς φασι
B Μέλητος καὶ Ἄνυτος. αὐτοὶ μὲν γὰρ οἱ διεφθαρμένοι
τάχ᾽ ἂν λόγον ἔχοιεν βοηθοῦντες· οἱ δὲ ἀδιάφθαρτοι,
πρεσβύτεροι ἤδη ἄνδρες, οἱ τούτων προσήκοντες, τίνα 40
ἄλλον ἔχουσι λόγον βοηθοῦντες ἐμοὶ ἀλλ᾽ ἢ τὸν ὀρθόν
τε καὶ δίκαιον, ὅτι ξυνίσασι Μελήτῳ μὲν ψευδομένῳ,
ἐμοὶ δὲ ἀληθεύοντι;

CONCLUDING REMARKS: XXIII–XXIV

XXIII. Εἶεν δή, ὦ ἄνδρες· ἃ μὲν ἐγὼ ἔχοιμ᾽ ἂν
ἀπολογεῖσθαι, σχεδόν ἐστι ταῦτα καὶ ἄλλα ἴσως
C τοιαῦτα. τάχα δ᾽ ἄν τις ὑμῶν ἀγανακτήσειεν ἀναμνησθεὶς ἑαυτοῦ, εἰ ὁ μὲν καὶ ἐλάττω τουτουῒ τοῦ ἀγῶνος
ἀγῶνα ἀγωνιζόμενος ἐδεήθη τε καὶ ἱκέτευσε τοὺς 5

δικαστὰς μετὰ πολλῶν δακρύων, παιδία τε αὐτοῦ
ἀναβιβασάμενος, ἵνα ὅ τι μάλιστα ἐλεηθείη, καὶ
ἄλλους τῶν οἰκείων καὶ φίλων πολλούς, ἐγὼ δὲ οὐδὲν
ἄρα τούτων ποιήσω, καὶ ταῦτα κινδυνεύων, ὡς ἂν
δόξαιμι, τὸν ἔσχατον κίνδυνον. τάχ᾽ οὖν τις ταῦτα 10
ἐννοήσας αὐθαδέστερον ἂν πρός με σχοίη, καὶ ὀργισ-
D θεὶς αὐτοῖς τούτοις θεῖτο ἂν μετ᾽ ὀργῆς τὴν ψῆφον. εἰ δή
τις ὑμῶν οὕτως ἔχει,—οὐκ ἀξιῶ μὲν γὰρ ἔγωγε· εἰ
δ᾽ οὖν, ἐπιεικῆ ἄν μοι δοκῶ πρὸς τοῦτον λέγειν λέγων ὅτι
Ἐμοί, ὦ ἄριστε, εἰσὶν μέν πού τινες καὶ οἰκεῖοι· καὶ 15
γάρ, τοῦτο αὐτὸ τὸ τοῦ Ὁμήρου, οὐδ᾽ ἐγὼ "ἀπὸ
δρυὸς οὐδ᾽ ἀπὸ πέτρης" πέφυκα, ἀλλ᾽ ἐξ ἀνθρώπων,
ὥστε καὶ οἰκεῖοί μοί εἰσι καὶ υἱεῖς, ὦ ἄνδρες Ἀθηναῖοι,
τρεῖς, εἷς μὲν μειράκιον ἤδη, δύο δὲ παιδία· ἀλλ᾽ ὅμως
οὐδέν᾽ αὐτῶν δεῦρο ἀναβιβασάμενος δεήσομαι ὑμῶν 20
ἀποψηφίσασθαι. τί δὴ οὖν οὐδὲν τούτων ποιήσω; οὐκ
E αὐθαδιζόμενος, ὦ ἄνδρες Ἀθηναῖοι, οὐδ᾽ ὑμᾶς ἀτιμάζων, ἀλλ᾽ εἰ μὲν θαρραλέως ἐγὼ ἔχω πρὸς θάνατον
ἢ μή, ἄλλος λόγος, πρὸς δ᾽ οὖν δόξαν καὶ ἐμοὶ καὶ
ὑμῖν καὶ ὅλῃ τῇ πόλει οὔ μοι δοκεῖ καλὸν εἶναι ἐμὲ 25
τούτων οὐδὲν ποιεῖν καὶ τηλικόνδε ὄντα καὶ τοῦτο
τοὔνομα ἔχοντα, εἴτ᾽ οὖν ἀληθὲς εἴτ᾽ οὖν ψεῦδος· ἀλλ᾽
οὖν δεδογμένον γέ ἐστι τὸν Σωκράτη διαφέρειν τινὶ
35 τῶν πολλῶν | ἀνθρώπων. εἰ οὖν ὑμῶν οἱ δοκοῦντες
διαφέρειν εἴτε σοφίᾳ εἴτε ἀνδρείᾳ εἴτε ἄλλῃ ᾑτινιοῦν 30
ἀρετῇ τοιοῦτοι ἔσονται, αἰσχρὸν ἂν εἴη· οἵουσπερ ἐγὼ
πολλάκις ἑώρακά τινας, ὅταν κρίνωνται, δοκοῦντας
μέν τι εἶναι, θαυμάσια δὲ ἐργαζομένους, ὡς δεινόν τι
οἰομένους πείσεσθαι εἰ ἀποθανοῦνται, ὥσπερ ἀθανάτων
ἐσομένων, ἂν ὑμεῖς αὐτοὺς μὴ ἀποκτείνητε· οἳ ἐμοὶ 35

δοκοῦσιν αἰσχύνην τῇ πόλει περιάπτειν, ὥστ' ἄν τινα
καὶ τῶν ξένων ὑπολαβεῖν ὅτι οἱ διαφέροντες Ἀθηναίων
B εἰς ἀρετήν, οὓς αὐτοὶ ἑαυτῶν ἔν τε ταῖς ἀρχαῖς καὶ ταῖς
ἄλλαις τιμαῖς προκρίνουσιν, οὗτοι γυναικῶν οὐδὲν
διαφέρουσιν. ταῦτα γάρ, ὦ ἄνδρες Ἀθηναῖοι, οὔτε 40
ὑμᾶς χρὴ ποιεῖν τοὺς δοκοῦντας καὶ ὁπηοῦν τι εἶναι,
οὔτ', ἂν ἡμεῖς ποιῶμεν, ὑμᾶς ἐπιτρέπειν, ἀλλὰ τοῦτο
αὐτὸ ἐνδείκνυσθαι, ὅτι πολὺ μᾶλλον καταψηφιεῖσθε τοῦ
τὰ ἐλεεινὰ ταῦτα δράματα εἰσάγοντος καὶ καταγέ-
λαστον τὴν πόλιν ποιοῦντος ἢ τοῦ ἡσυχίαν ἄγοντος.   45

XXIV. Χωρὶς δὲ τῆς δόξης, ὦ ἄνδρες, οὐδὲ
C δίκαιόν μοι δοκεῖ εἶναι δεῖσθαι τοῦ δικαστοῦ οὐδὲ
δεόμενον ἀποφεύγειν, ἀλλὰ διδάσκειν καὶ πείθειν. οὐ
γὰρ ἐπὶ τούτῳ κάθηται ὁ δικαστής, ἐπὶ τῷ καταχαρίζεσθαι τὰ δίκαια, ἀλλ' ἐπὶ τῷ κρίνειν ταῦτα· καὶ 5
ὀμώμοκεν οὐ χαριεῖσθαι οἷς ἂν δοκῇ αὐτῷ, ἀλλὰ
δικάσειν κατὰ τοὺς νόμους. οὔκουν χρὴ οὔτε ἡμᾶς
ἐθίζειν ὑμᾶς ἐπιορκεῖν, οὔθ' ὑμᾶς ἐθίζεσθαι· οὐδέτεροι
γὰρ ἂν ἡμῶν εὐσεβοῖεν. μὴ οὖν ἀξιοῦτέ με, ὦ ἄνδρες
Ἀθηναῖοι, τοιαῦτα δεῖν πρὸς ὑμᾶς πράττειν, ἃ μήτε 10
D ἡγοῦμαι καλὰ εἶναι μήτε δίκαια μήτε ὅσια, ἄλλως τε
μέντοι νὴ Δία πάντως καὶ ἀσεβείας φεύγοντα ὑπὸ
Μελήτου τουτουί. σαφῶς γὰρ ἄν, εἰ πείθοιμι ὑμᾶς καὶ
τῷ δεῖσθαι βιαζοίμην ὀμωμοκότας, θεοὺς ἂν διδά-
σκοιμι μὴ ἡγεῖσθαι ὑμᾶς εἶναι, καὶ ἀτεχνῶς ἀπολογού- 15
μενος κατηγοροίην ἂν ἐμαυτοῦ ὡς θεοὺς οὐ νομίζω.
ἀλλὰ πολλοῦ δεῖ οὕτως ἔχειν· νομίζω τε γάρ, ὦ
ἄνδρες Ἀθηναῖοι, ὡς οὐδεὶς τῶν ἐμῶν κατηγόρων, καὶ
ὑμῖν ἐπιτρέπω καὶ τῷ θεῷ κρῖναι περὶ ἐμοῦ ὅπη
μέλλει ἐμοί τε ἄριστα εἶναι καὶ ὑμῖν.   20

PART II. AFTER THE VERDICT
AND BEFORE THE SENTENCE

(Second Speech)

CHAPTERS XXV–XXVIII

E   **XXV.** Τὸ μὲν μὴ ἀγανακτεῖν, ὦ ἄνδρες Ἀθηναῖοι,
36 ἐπὶ | τούτῳ τῷ γεγονότι, ὅτι μου κατεψηφίσασθε,
ἄλλα τέ μοι πολλὰ ξυμβάλλεται, καὶ οὐκ ἀνέλπιστόν
μοι γέγονεν τὸ γεγονὸς τοῦτο, ἀλλὰ πολὺ μᾶλλον
θαυμάζω ἑκατέρων τῶν ψήφων τὸν γεγονότα ἀριθμόν. 5
οὐ γὰρ ᾠόμην ἔγωγε οὕτω παρ' ὀλίγον ἔσεσθαι ἀλλὰ
παρὰ πολύ· νῦν δέ, ὡς ἔοικεν, εἰ τριάκοντα μόναι
μετέπεσον τῶν ψήφων, ἀπεπεφεύγη ἄν. Μέλητον μὲν
οὖν, ὡς ἐμοὶ δοκῶ, καὶ νῦν ἀποπέφευγα, καὶ οὐ μόνον
ἀποπέφευγα, ἀλλὰ παντὶ δῆλον τοῦτό γε, ὅτι, εἰ μὴ 10
ἀνέβη Ἄνυτος καὶ Λύκων κατηγορήσοντες ἐμοῦ, κἂν
B ὦφλε χιλίας δραχμάς, οὐ μεταλαβὼν τὸ πέμπτον μέρος
τῶν ψήφων.

    XXVI. Τιμᾶται δ' οὖν μοι ὁ ἀνὴρ θανάτου. εἶεν·
ἐγὼ δὲ δὴ τίνος ὑμῖν ἀντιτιμήσομαι, ὦ ἄνδρες Ἀθηναῖοι; ἢ δῆλον ὅτι τῆς ἀξίας; τί οὖν; τί ἄξιός εἰμι
παθεῖν ἢ ἀποτῖσαι, ὅ τι μαθὼν ἐν τῷ βίῳ οὐχ ἡσυχίαν
ἦγον, ἀλλ' ἀμελήσας ὧνπερ οἱ πολλοί, χρηματισμοῦ 5
τε καὶ οἰκονομίας καὶ στρατηγιῶν καὶ δημηγοριῶν καὶ
τῶν ἄλλων, ἀρχῶν καὶ ξυνωμοσιῶν καὶ στάσεων, τῶν
ἐν τῇ πόλει γιγνομένων, ἡγησάμενος ἐμαυτὸν τῷ ὄντι
C ἐπιεικέστερον εἶναι ἢ ὥστε εἰς ταῦτ' ἰόντα σῴζεσθαι,
ἐνταῦθα μὲν οὐκ ᾖα, οἷ ἐλθὼν μήτε ὑμῖν μήτε ἐμαυτῷ 10

ἔμελλον μηδὲν ὄφελος εἶναι, ἐπὶ δὲ τὸ ἰδίᾳ ἕκαστον ἰὼν
εὐεργετεῖν τὴν μεγίστην εὐεργεσίαν, ὡς ἐγώ φημι,
ἐνταῦθα ᾖα, ἐπιχειρῶν ἕκαστον ὑμῶν πείθειν μὴ
πρότερον μήτε τῶν ἑαυτοῦ μηδενὸς ἐπιμελεῖσθαι, πρὶν
ἑαυτοῦ ἐπιμεληθείη, ὅπως ὡς βέλτιστος καὶ φρονιμώ- 15
τατος ἔσοιτο, μήτε τῶν τῆς πόλεως, πρὶν αὐτῆς τῆς
πόλεως, τῶν τε ἄλλων οὕτω κατὰ τὸν αὐτὸν τρόπον
D ἐπιμελεῖσθαι· τί οὖν εἰμι ἄξιος παθεῖν τοιοῦτος ὤν;
ἀγαθόν τι, ὦ ἄνδρες Ἀθηναῖοι, εἰ δεῖ γε κατὰ τὴν
ἀξίαν τῇ ἀληθείᾳ τιμᾶσθαι· καὶ ταῦτά γε ἀγαθὸν 20
τοιοῦτον, ὅ τι ἂν πρέποι ἐμοί. τί οὖν πρέπει ἀνδρὶ
πένητι εὐεργέτῃ, δεομένῳ ἄγειν σχολὴν ἐπὶ τῇ ὑμε-
τέρᾳ παρακελεύσει; οὐκ ἔσθ' ὅ τι μᾶλλον, ὦ ἄνδρες
Ἀθηναῖοι, πρέπει [οὕτως], ὡς τὸν τοιοῦτον ἄνδρα ἐν
πρυτανείῳ σιτεῖσθαι, πολύ γε μᾶλλον ἢ εἴ τις ὑμῶν 25
ἵππῳ ἢ ξυνωρίδι ἢ ζεύγει νενίκηκεν Ὀλυμπίασιν.
ὁ μὲν γὰρ ὑμᾶς ποιεῖ εὐδαίμονας δοκεῖν εἶναι, ἐγὼ
E δὲ εἶναι· καὶ ὁ μὲν τροφῆς οὐδὲν δεῖται, ἐγὼ δὲ δέομαι.
εἰ οὖν δεῖ με κατὰ τὸ δίκαιον τῆς ἀξίας τιμᾶσθαι,
37 τούτου | τιμῶμαι, ἐν πρυτανείῳ σιτήσεως.   30

XXVII. Ἴσως οὖν ὑμῖν καὶ ταυτὶ λέγων παρα-
πλησίως δοκῶ λέγειν ὥσπερ περὶ τοῦ οἴκτου καὶ τῆς
ἀντιβολήσεως, ἀπαυθαδιζόμενος· τὸ δὲ οὐκ ἔστιν, ὦ
Ἀθηναῖοι, τοιοῦτον, ἀλλὰ τοιόνδε μᾶλλον. πέπεισμαι
ἐγὼ ἑκὼν εἶναι μηδένα ἀδικεῖν ἀνθρώπων, ἀλλὰ ὑμᾶς 5
τοῦτο οὐ πείθω· ὀλίγον γάρ χρόνον ἀλλήλοις διει-
λέγμεθα· ἐπεί, ὡς ἐγῷμαι, εἰ ἦν ὑμῖν νόμος, ὥσπερ καὶ
B ἄλλοις ἀνθρώποις, περὶ θανάτου μὴ μίαν ἡμέραν μόνον
κρίνειν, ἀλλὰ πολλάς, ἐπείσθητε ἄν· νῦν δ' οὐ ῥᾴδιον
ἐν χρόνῳ ὀλίγῳ μεγάλας διαβολὰς ἀπολύεσθαι. 10

4   49   AAS

πεπεισμένος δὴ ἐγὼ μηδένα ἀδικεῖν πολλοῦ δέω
ἐμαυτόν γε ἀδικήσειν καὶ κατ' ἐμαυτοῦ ἐρεῖν αὐτός, ὡς
ἄξιός εἰμί του κακοῦ, καὶ τιμήσεσθαι τοιούτου τινὸς
ἐμαυτῷ. τί δείσας; ἢ μὴ πάθω τοῦτο, οὗ Μέλητός μοι
τιμᾶται, ὅ φημι οὐκ εἰδέναι οὔτ' εἰ ἀγαθὸν οὔτ' εἰ 15
κακόν ἐστιν; ἀντὶ τούτου δὴ ἕλωμαι ὧν εὖ οἶδ' ὅτι
C κακῶν ὄντων; τοῦ τιμησάμενος; πότερον δεσμοῦ; καὶ
τί με δεῖ ζῆν ἐν δεσμωτηρίῳ, δουλεύοντα τῇ ἀεὶ
καθισταμένῃ ἀρχῇ, τοῖς ἕνδεκα; ἀλλὰ χρημάτων, καὶ
δεδέσθαι ἕως ἂν ἐκτίσω; ἀλλὰ ταὐτόν μοί ἐστιν, ὅπερ 20
νῦν δὴ ἔλεγον· οὐ γὰρ ἔστι μοι χρήματα, ὁπόθεν
ἐκτίσω. ἀλλὰ δὴ φυγῆς τιμήσωμαι; ἴσως γὰρ ἂν μοι
τούτου τιμήσαιτε. πολλὴ μεντἂν με φιλοψυχία ἔχοι,
εἰ οὕτως ἀλόγιστός εἰμι ὥστε μὴ δύνασθαι λογίζεσθαι,
ὅτι ὑμεῖς μὲν ὄντες πολῖταί μου οὐχ οἷοί τε ἐγένεσθε 25
D ἐνεγκεῖν τὰς ἐμὰς διατριβὰς καὶ τοὺς λόγους, ἀλλ'
ὑμῖν βαρύτεραι γεγόνασιν καὶ ἐπιφθονώτεραι, ὥστε
ζητεῖτε αὐτῶν νυνὶ ἀπαλλαγῆναι, ἄλλοι δὲ ἄρα αὐτὰς
οἴσουσι ῥᾳδίως; πολλοῦ γε δεῖ, ὦ Ἀθηναῖοι. καλὸς
οὖν ἄν μοι ὁ βίος εἴη ἐξελθόντι, τηλικῷδε ἀνθρώπῳ 30
ἄλλην ἐξ ἄλλης πόλεως ἀμειβομένῳ καὶ ἐξελαυνομένῳ
ζῆν. εὖ γὰρ οἶδ' ὅτι, ὅποι ἂν ἔλθω, λέγοντος ἐμοῦ
ἀκροάσονται οἱ νέοι ὥσπερ ἐνθάδε· κἂν μὲν τούτους
E ἀπελαύνω, οὗτοι ἐμὲ αὐτοὶ ἐξελῶσι, πείθοντες τοὺς
πρεσβυτέρους· ἐὰν δὲ μὴ ἀπελαύνω, οἱ τούτων 35
πατέρες τε καὶ οἰκεῖοι δι' αὐτοὺς τούτους.

XXVIII. Ἴσως οὖν ἄν τις εἴποι· Σιγῶν δὲ καὶ
ἡσυχίαν ἄγων, ὦ Σώκρατες, οὐχ οἷός τ' ἔσει ἡμῖν
ἐξελθὼν ζῆν; τουτὶ δή ἐστι πάντων χαλεπώτατον
πεῖσαί τινας ὑμῶν. ἐάν τε γὰρ λέγω ὅτι τῷ θεῷ

ἀπειθεῖν τοῦτ' ἐστὶν καὶ διὰ τοῦτο ἀδύνατον ἡσυχίαν 5
38 ἄγειν, οὐ πείσεσθέ μοι ὡς εἰρωνευομένῳ · | ἐάν τ' αὖ
λέγω ὅτι καὶ τυγχάνει μέγιστον ἀγαθὸν ὂν ἀνθρώπῳ
τοῦτο, ἑκάστης ἡμέρας περὶ ἀρετῆς τοὺς λόγους
ποιεῖσθαι καὶ τῶν ἄλλων, περὶ ὧν ὑμεῖς ἐμοῦ ἀκούετε
διαλεγομένου καὶ ἐμαυτὸν καὶ ἄλλους ἐξετάζοντος, ὁ 10
δὲ ἀνεξέταστος βίος οὐ βιωτὸς ἀνθρώπῳ, ταῦτα δ' ἔτι
ἧττον πείσεσθέ μοι λέγοντι. τὰ δὲ ἔχει μὲν οὕτως, ὡς
ἐγώ φημι, ὦ ἄνδρες, πείθειν δὲ οὐ ῥᾴδιον. καὶ ἐγὼ
ἅμα οὐκ εἴθισμαι ἐμαυτὸν ἀξιοῦν κακοῦ οὐδενός. εἰ
B μὲν γὰρ ἦν μοι χρήματα, ἐτιμησάμην ἂν χρημάτων 15
ὅσα ἔμελλον ἐκτίσειν · οὐδὲν γὰρ ἂν ἐβλάβην · νῦν δέ—
οὐ γὰρ ἔστιν, εἰ μὴ ἄρα ὅσον ἂν ἐγὼ δυναίμην ἐκτῖσαι,
τοσούτου βούλεσθέ μοι τιμῆσαι. ἴσως δ' ἂν δυναίμην
ἐκτῖσαι ὑμῖν μνᾶν ἀργυρίου · τοσούτου οὖν τιμῶμαι.
Πλάτων δὲ ὅδε, ὦ ἄνδρες Ἀθηναῖοι, καὶ Κρίτων καὶ 20
Κριτόβουλος καὶ Ἀπολλόδωρος κελεύουσί με τριάκοντα μνῶν τιμήσασθαι, αὐτοὶ δ' ἐγγυᾶσθαι · τιμῶμαι
οὖν τοσούτου, ἐγγυηταὶ δ' ὑμῖν ἔσονται τοῦ ἀργυρίου
οὗτοι ἀξιόχρεῳ.

PART III. AFTER THE SENTENCE

(*Third Speech*)

CHAPTERS XXIX–XXXIII

(*a*) To those who voted for the death-penalty (XXIX–XXX).

(*b*) To those who voted against it (XXXI–XXXII).

(*c*) Conclusion (XXXII).

C XXIX. Οὐ πολλοῦ γ' ἕνεκα χρόνου, ὦ ἄνδρες
Ἀθηναῖοι, ὄνομα ἕξετε καὶ αἰτίαν ὑπὸ τῶν βουλο-
μένων τὴν πόλιν λοιδορεῖν, ὡς Σωκράτη ἀπεκτόνατε,
ἄνδρα σοφόν· φήσουσι γὰρ δή με σοφὸν εἶναι, εἰ καὶ
μὴ εἰμί, οἱ βουλόμενοι ὑμῖν ὀνειδίζειν. εἰ οὖν περι- 5
εμείνατε ὀλίγον χρόνον, ἀπὸ τοῦ αὐτομάτου ἂν ὑμῖν
τοῦτο ἐγένετο· ὁρᾶτε γὰρ δὴ τὴν ἡλικίαν, ὅτι πόρρω
D ἤδη ἐστὶ τοῦ βίου, θανάτου δὲ ἐγγύς. λέγω δὲ τοῦτο οὐ
πρὸς πάντας ὑμᾶς, ἀλλὰ πρὸς τοὺς ἐμοῦ καταψηφισα-
μένους θάνατον. λέγω δὲ καὶ τόδε πρὸς τοὺς αὐτοὺς 10
τούτους. ἴσως με οἴεσθε, ὦ ἄνδρες, ἀπορίᾳ λόγων
ἑαλωκέναι τοιούτων, οἷς ἂν ὑμᾶς ἔπεισα, εἰ ᾤμην δεῖν
ἅπαντα ποιεῖν καὶ λέγειν, ὥστε ἀποφυγεῖν τὴν δίκην.
πολλοῦ γε δεῖ. ἀλλ' ἀπορίᾳ μὲν ἑάλωκα, οὐ μέντοι
λόγων, ἀλλὰ τόλμης καὶ ἀναισχυντίας καὶ τοῦ ἐθέλειν 15
λέγειν πρὸς ὑμᾶς τοιαῦτα, οἷ' ἂν ὑμῖν ἥδιστα ἦν
ἀκούειν, θρηνοῦντός τέ μου καὶ ὀδυρομένου καὶ ἄλλα
E ποιοῦντος καὶ λέγοντος πολλὰ καὶ ἀνάξια ἐμοῦ, ὡς
ἐγώ φημι· οἷα δὴ καὶ εἴθισθε ὑμεῖς τῶν ἄλλων
ἀκούειν. ἀλλ' οὔτε τότε ᾠήθην δεῖν ἕνεκα τοῦ κινδύνου 20
πρᾶξαι οὐδὲν ἀνελεύθερον, οὔτε νῦν μοι μεταμέλει

οὕτως ἀπολογησαμένῳ, ἀλλὰ πολὺ μᾶλλον αἱροῦμαι
ὧδε ἀπολογησάμενος τεθνάναι ἢ ἐκείνως ζῆν· οὔτε γὰρ
ἐν δίκῃ οὔτ᾽ ἐν πολέμῳ οὔτ᾽ ἐμὲ οὔτ᾽ ἄλλον οὐδένα δεῖ
39 τοῦτο | μηχανᾶσθαι, ὅπως ἀποφεύξεται πᾶν ποιῶν 25
θάνατον. καὶ γὰρ ἐν ταῖς μάχαις πολλάκις δῆλον
γίγνεται ὅτι τό γε ἀποθανεῖν ἄν τις ἐκφύγοι καὶ ὅπλα
ἀφεὶς καὶ ἐφ᾽ ἱκετείαν τραπόμενος τῶν διωκόντων· καὶ
ἄλλαι μηχαναὶ πολλαί εἰσιν ἐν ἑκάστοις τοῖς κινδύνοις,
ὥστε διαφεύγειν θάνατον, ἐάν τις τολμᾷ πᾶν ποιεῖν καὶ 30
λέγειν. ἀλλὰ μὴ οὐ τοῦτ᾽ ᾖ χαλεπόν, ὦ ἄνδρες,
θάνατον ἐκφυγεῖν, ἀλλὰ πολὺ χαλεπώτερον πονηρίαν·
B θᾶττον γὰρ θανάτου θεῖ. καὶ νῦν ἐγὼ μὲν ἅτε βραδὺς
ὢν καὶ πρεσβύτης ὑπὸ τοῦ βραδυτέρου ἑάλων, οἱ δ᾽
ἐμοὶ κατήγοροι ἅτε δεινοὶ καὶ ὀξεῖς ὄντες ὑπὸ τοῦ 35
θάττονος, τῆς κακίας. καὶ νῦν ἐγὼ μὲν ἄπειμι ὑφ᾽
ὑμῶν θανάτου δίκην ὀφλών, οὗτοι δ᾽ ὑπὸ τῆς ἀληθείας
ὠφληκότες μοχθηρίαν καὶ ἀδικίαν. καὶ ἐγώ τε τῷ
τιμήματι ἐμμένω καὶ οὗτοι. ταῦτα μέν που ἴσως
οὕτως καὶ ἔδει σχεῖν, καὶ οἶμαι αὐτὰ μετρίως ἔχειν. 40
XXX. Τὸ δὲ δὴ μετὰ τοῦτο ἐπιθυμῶ ὑμῖν
C χρησμῳδῆσαι, ὦ καταψηφισάμενοί μου· καὶ γάρ εἰμι
ἤδη ἐνταῦθα, ἐν ᾧ μάλιστα ἄνθρωποι χρησμῳδοῦσιν,
ὅταν μέλλωσιν ἀποθανεῖσθαι. φημὶ γάρ, ὦ ἄνδρες, οἳ
ἐμὲ ἀπεκτόνατε, τιμωρίαν ὑμῖν ἥξειν εὐθὺς μετὰ τὸν 5
ἐμὸν θάνατον πολὺ χαλεπωτέραν νὴ Δία ἢ οἵαν ἐμὲ
ἀπεκτόνατε· νῦν γὰρ τοῦτο εἰργάσασθε οἰόμενοι μὲν
ἀπαλλάξεσθαι τοῦ διδόναι ἔλεγχον τοῦ βίου, τὸ δὲ
ὑμῖν πολὺ ἐναντίον ἀποβήσεται, ὡς ἐγώ φημι. πλείους
ἔσονται ὑμᾶς οἱ ἐλέγχοντες, οὓς νῦν ἐγὼ κατεῖχον, 10
D ὑμεῖς δὲ οὐκ ᾐσθάνεσθε· καὶ χαλεπώτεροι ἔσονται

53

ὅσῳ νεώτεροί εἰσιν, καὶ ὑμεῖς μᾶλλον ἀγανακτήσετε.
εἰ γὰρ οἴεσθε ἀποκτείνοντες ἀνθρώπους ἐπισχήσειν τοῦ
ὀνειδίζειν τινὰ ὑμῖν ὅτι οὐκ ὀρθῶς ζῆτε, οὐκ ὀρθῶς
διανοεῖσθε· οὐ γάρ ἐσθ᾽ αὕτη ἡ ἀπαλλαγὴ οὔτε πάνυ 15
δυνατὴ οὔτε καλή, ἀλλ᾽ ἐκείνη καὶ καλλίστη καὶ
ῥᾴστη, μὴ τοὺς ἄλλους κολούειν, ἀλλ᾽ ἑαυτὸν παρα-
σκευάζειν ὅπως ἔσται ὡς βέλτιστος. ταῦτα μὲν οὖν
ὑμῖν τοῖς καταψηφισαμένοις μαντευσάμενος ἀπαλ-
λάττομαι.   20

E XXXI. Τοῖς δὲ ἀποψηφισαμένοις ἡδέως ἂν δια-
λεχθείην ὑπὲρ τοῦ γεγονότος τουτουὶ πράγματος, ἐν ᾧ
οἱ ἄρχοντες ἀσχολίαν ἄγουσι καὶ οὔπω ἔρχομαι οἷ
ἐλθόντα με δεῖ τεθνάναι. ἀλλά μοι, ὦ ἄνδρες, παρα-
μείνατε τοσοῦτον χρόνον· οὐδὲν γὰρ κωλύει δια- 5
μυθολογῆσαι πρὸς ἀλλήλους, ἕως ἔξεστιν. ὑμῖν γὰρ
40 ὡς | φίλοις οὖσιν ἐπιδεῖξαι ἐθέλω τὸ νυνί μοι ξυμβε-
βηκὸς τί ποτε νοεῖ. ἐμοὶ γάρ, ὦ ἄνδρες δικασταί—
ὑμᾶς γὰρ δικαστὰς καλῶν ὀρθῶς ἂν καλοίην—
θαυμάσιόν τι γέγονεν. ἡ γὰρ εἰωθυῖά μοι μαντικὴ ἡ 10
τοῦ δαιμονίου ἐν μὲν τῷ πρόσθεν χρόνῳ παντὶ πάνυ
πυκνὴ ἀεὶ ἦν καὶ πάνυ ἐπὶ σμικροῖς ἐναντιουμένη, εἴ
τι μέλλοιμι μὴ ὀρθῶς πράξειν. νυνὶ δὲ ξυμβέβηκέ μοι,
ἅπερ ὁρᾶτε καὶ αὐτοί, ταυτὶ ἅ γε δὴ οἰηθείη ἄν τις καὶ
B νομίζεται ἔσχατα κακῶν εἶναι. ἐμοὶ δὲ οὔτε ἐξιόντι 15
ἕωθεν οἴκοθεν ἠναντιώθη τὸ τοῦ θεοῦ σημεῖον, οὔτε
ἡνίκα ἀνέβαινον ἐνταυθοῖ ἐπὶ τὸ δικαστήριον, οὔτε ἐν
τῷ λόγῳ οὐδαμοῦ μέλλοντί τι ἐρεῖν· καί τοι ἐν ἄλλοις
λόγοις πολλαχοῦ δή με ἐπέσχε λέγοντα μεταξύ· νῦν
δὲ οὐδαμοῦ περὶ ταύτην τὴν πρᾶξιν οὔτ᾽ ἐν ἔργῳ 20
οὐδενὶ οὔτ᾽ ἐν λόγῳ ἠναντίωταί μοι. τί οὖν αἴτιον

εἶναι ὑπολαμβάνω; ἐγὼ ὑμῖν ἐρῶ· κινδυνεύει γάρ μοι
τὸ ξυμβεβηκὸς τοῦτο ἀγαθὸν γεγονέναι, καὶ οὐκ ἔσθ'
C ὅπως ἡμεῖς ὀρθῶς ὑπολαμβάνομεν, ὅσοι οἰόμεθα κακὸν
εἶναι τὸ τεθνάναι. μέγα μοι τεκμήριον τούτου 25
γέγονεν· οὐ γὰρ ἔσθ' ὅπως οὐκ ἠναντιώθη ἄν μοι τὸ
εἰωθὸς σημεῖον, εἰ μή τι ἔμελλον ἐγὼ ἀγαθὸν πράξειν.

XXXII. Ἐννοήσωμεν δὲ καὶ τῇδε, ὡς πολλὴ
ἐλπίς ἐστιν ἀγαθὸν αὐτὸ εἶναι. δυοῖν γὰρ θάτερόν
ἐστι τὸ τεθνάναι· ἢ γὰρ οἷον μηδὲν εἶναι, μηδὲ
αἴσθησιν μηδεμίαν μηδενὸς ἔχειν τὸν τεθνεῶτα, ἢ
κατὰ τὰ λεγόμενα μεταβολή τις τυγχάνει οὖσα καὶ 5
μετοίκησις τῇ ψυχῇ τοῦ τόπου τοῦ ἐνθένδε εἰς ἄλλον
D τόπον. καὶ εἴτε μηδεμία αἴσθησίς ἐστιν, ἀλλ' οἷον
ὕπνος, ἐπειδάν τις καθεύδων μηδ' ὄναρ μηδὲν ὁρᾷ,
θαυμάσιον κέρδος ἂν εἴη ὁ θάνατος. ἐγὼ γὰρ ἂν
οἶμαι, εἴ τινα ἐκλεξάμενον δέοι ταύτην τὴν νύκτα, ἐν 10
ᾗ οὕτω κατέδαρθεν, ὥστε μηδὲ ὄναρ ἰδεῖν, καὶ τὰς
ἄλλας νύκτας τε καὶ ἡμέρας τὰς τοῦ βίου τοῦ ἑαυτοῦ
ἀντιπαραθέντα ταύτῃ τῇ νυκτὶ δέοι σκεψάμενον εἰπεῖν,
πόσας ἄμεινον καὶ ἥδιον ἡμέρας καὶ νύκτας ταύτης τῆς
νυκτὸς βεβίωκεν ἐν τῷ ἑαυτοῦ βίῳ, οἶμαι ἂν μὴ ὅτι 15
E ἰδιώτην τινά, ἀλλὰ τὸν μέγαν βασιλέα εὐαριθμήτους ἂν
εὑρεῖν αὐτὸν ταύτας πρὸς τὰς ἄλλας ἡμέρας καὶ νύκτας.
εἰ οὖν τοιοῦτον ὁ θάνατός ἐστιν, κέρδος ἔγωγε λέγω·
καὶ γὰρ οὐδὲν πλεῖον ὁ πᾶς χρόνος φαίνεται οὕτω
δὴ εἶναι ἢ μία νύξ. εἰ δ' αὖ οἷον ἀποδημῆσαί ἐστιν ὁ 20
θάνατος ἐνθένδε εἰς ἄλλον τόπον, καὶ ἀληθῆ ἐστιν τὰ
λεγόμενα, ὡς ἄρα ἐκεῖ εἰσὶν ἅπαντες οἱ τεθνεῶτες, τί
μεῖζον ἀγαθὸν τούτου εἴη ἄν, ὦ ἄνδρες δικασταί; εἰ
γάρ τις ἀφικόμενος εἰς Ἅιδου, ἀπαλλαγεὶς τούτων |

41 τῶν φασκόντων δικαστῶν εἶναι, εὑρήσει τοὺς ἀληθῶς 25
δικαστάς, οἵπερ καὶ λέγονται ἐκεῖ δικάζειν, Μίνως τε
καὶ Ῥαδάμανθυς καὶ Αἰακὸς καὶ Τριπτόλεμος, καὶ
ἄλλοι ὅσοι τῶν ἡμιθέων δίκαιοι ἐγένοντο ἐν τῷ ἑαυτῶν
βίῳ, ἆρα φαύλη ἂν εἴη ἡ ἀποδημία; ἢ αὖ Ὀρφεῖ
ξυγγενέσθαι καὶ Μουσαίῳ καὶ Ἡσιόδῳ καὶ Ὁμήρῳ ἐπὶ 30
πόσῳ ἄν τις δέξαιτ' ἂν ὑμῶν; ἐγὼ μὲν γὰρ πολλάκις
θέλω τεθνάναι, εἰ ταῦτ' ἐστὶν ἀληθῆ· ἐπεὶ ἔμοιγε καὶ
B αὐτῷ θαυμαστὴ ἂν εἴη ἡ διατριβὴ αὐτόθι, ὁπότε ἐντύ-
χοιμι Παλαμήδει καὶ Αἴαντι τῷ Τελαμῶνος καὶ εἴ τις
ἄλλος τῶν παλαιῶν διὰ κρίσιν ἄδικον τέθνηκεν· 35
ἀντιπαραβάλλοντι τὰ ἐμαυτοῦ πάθη πρὸς τὰ ἐκείνων,
ὡς ἐγὼ οἶμαι, οὐκ ἂν ἀηδὲς εἴη. καὶ δὴ καὶ τὸ
μέγιστον, τοὺς ἐκεῖ ἐξετάζοντα καὶ ἐρευνῶντα ὥσπερ
τοὺς ἐνταῦθα διάγειν, τίς αὐτῶν σοφός ἐστιν καὶ τίς
οἴεται μέν, ἔστιν δ' οὔ. ἐπὶ πόσῳ δ' ἄν τις, ὦ ἄνδρες 40
δικασταί, δέξαιτο ἐξετάσαι τὸν ἐπὶ Τροίαν ἀγαγόντα
C τὴν πολλὴν στρατιὰν ἢ Ὀδυσσέα ἢ Σίσυφον; ἢ ἄλλους
μυρίους ἄν τις εἴποι καὶ ἄνδρας καὶ γυναῖκας, οἷς
ἐκεῖ διαλέγεσθαι καὶ ξυνεῖναι καὶ ἐξετάζειν ἀμήχανον
ἂν εἴη εὐδαιμονίας. πάντως οὐ δήπου τούτου γε 45
ἕνεκα οἱ ἐκεῖ ἀποκτείνουσι· τά τε γὰρ ἄλλα εὐδαι-
μονέστεροί εἰσιν οἱ ἐκεῖ τῶν ἐνθάδε, καὶ ἤδη τὸν
λοιπὸν χρόνον ἀθάνατοί εἰσιν, εἴπερ γε τὰ λεγόμενα
ἀληθῆ ἐστίν.

XXXIII. Ἀλλὰ καὶ ὑμᾶς χρή, ὦ ἄνδρες δικασταί,
εὐέλπιδας εἶναι πρὸς τὸν θάνατον, καὶ ἕν τι τοῦτο
D διανοεῖσθαι ἀληθές, ὅτι οὐκ ἔστιν ἀνδρὶ ἀγαθῷ κακὸν
οὐδὲν οὔτε ζῶντι οὔτε τελευτήσαντι, οὐδὲ ἀμελεῖται
ὑπὸ θεῶν τὰ τούτου πράγματα· οὐδὲ τὰ ἐμὰ νῦν ἀπὸ 5

τοῦ αὐτομάτου γέγονεν, ἀλλά μοι δῆλόν ἐστι τοῦτο, ὅτι
ἤδη τεθνάναι καὶ ἀπηλλάχθαι πραγμάτων βέλτιον ἦν
μοι. διὰ τοῦτο καὶ ἐμὲ οὐδαμοῦ ἀπέτρεψεν τὸ σημεῖον,
καὶ ἔγωγε τοῖς καταψηφισαμένοις μου καὶ τοῖς
κατηγόροις οὐ πάνυ χαλεπαίνω. καί τοι οὐ ταύτῃ τῇ 10
διανοίᾳ κατεψηφίζοντό μου καὶ κατηγόρουν, ἀλλ᾽
οἰόμενοι βλάπτειν· τοῦτο αὐτοῖς ἄξιον μέμφεσθαι.
Ε τοσόνδε μέντοι αὐτῶν δέομαι· τοὺς υἱεῖς μου, ἐπειδὰν
ἡβήσωσι, τιμωρήσασθε, ὦ ἄνδρες, ταὐτὰ ταῦτα
λυποῦντες, ἅπερ ἐγὼ ὑμᾶς ἐλύπουν, ἐὰν ὑμῖν δοκῶσιν 15
ἢ χρημάτων ἢ ἄλλου του πρότερον ἐπιμελεῖσθαι ἢ
ἀρετῆς, καὶ ἐὰν δοκῶσί τι εἶναι μηδὲν ὄντες, ὀνειδίζετε
αὐτοῖς, ὥσπερ ἐγὼ ὑμῖν, ὅτι οὐκ ἐπιμελοῦνται ὧν δεῖ,
καὶ οἴονταί τι εἶναι ὄντες οὐδενὸς ἄξιοι. καὶ ἐὰν ταῦτα
42 ποιῆτε, δίκαια | πεπονθὼς ἐγὼ ἔσομαι ὑφ᾽ ὑμῶν αὐτός 20
τε καὶ οἱ υἱεῖς. ἀλλὰ γὰρ ἤδη ὥρα ἀπιέναι, ἐμοὶ μὲν
ἀποθανουμένῳ, ὑμῖν δὲ βιωσομένοις· ὁπότεροι δὲ
ἡμῶν ἔρχονται ἐπὶ ἄμεινον πρᾶγμα, ἄδηλον παντὶ πλὴν
ἢ τῷ θεῷ.

NOTES

PART I

Before the Verdict

(First Speech)

CHAPTER I

[17A] 1 **ὅ τι μὲν ὑμεῖς—κατηγόρων -** 'What impression has been made on you by my accusers', lit. 'What you have been made (in your feelings) by my accusers.' πάσχειν, 'to suffer', 'to be treated'. perf. πέπονθα, serves as the passive to ποιεῖν, 'to make', 'to do'.

2 **δ' οὖν -** 'at all events'. **καὶ αὐτός**, 'for my part'. **ὀλίγου** used adverbially = 'within a little', 'almost'. So, too, ὀλίγου δεῖν (22A).

4 **ὡς ἔπος εἰπεῖν** is to be taken with οὐδέν. The phrase is equivalent to Lat. *paene dixerim*, and is used to soften the universal words οὐδείς, πᾶς. οὐδὲν ὡς ἔπος εἰπεῖν = 'hardly anything'; πᾶν ὡς ἔπος εἰπεῖν = 'nearly everything'.

5 **αὐτῶν ἕν ἐθαύμασα -** αὐτῶν is masc. 'I wondered at one thing in them.' This is a common construction of θαυμάζω, but we also find θαυμάζω τινά τινος (neut.) 'I admire somebody *for* something'.

τῶν πολλῶν ὧν - In Greek where we should expect to find a relative pronoun in the accusative (here ἅ instead of ὧν ἐψεύσαντο), the case of the antecedent is generally used. This happens most often when the antecedent is in the genitive, not infrequently also when it is in the dative case, and the relative pronoun is commonly said to be 'attracted' to its antecedent.

[17B] 10 **τοῦτο** sums up the whole of the preceding clauses τὸ γὰρ—λέγειν, which together form the subject to ἔδοξεν. 'The fact that they were not ashamed', etc.—'*this* seemed to me'.

11 **αὐτῶν -** 'In them', like αὐτῶν ἕν ἐθαύμασα above.

εἰ μὴ ἄρα - ἄρα is ironical, 'unless indeed', Lat. *nisi forte*.

13 **λέγουσιν** = 'mean'. **οὐ κατὰ τούτους**, 'not after their style'.

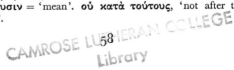

14 ἤ τι ἤ οὐδέν - 'little or nothing', lit. 'either something or nothing'. The phrase is common.

17 ὥσπερ οἱ τούτων - Supply λόγοι κεκαλλιέπηνται.

18 ῥήμασί τε καὶ ὀνόμασιν - 'With words and 'phrases.'

[17 C] 19 τοῖς ἐπιτυχοῦσιν ὀνόμασιν - 'In any words that come to me.' ἐπιτυγχάνειν = 'to meet'; Socrates regards the words of his defence metaphorically as casual visitors to him from outside, not as the fruits of a search for the right expression.

22 τῇδε τῇ ἡλικίᾳ - 'for a man of my age'. πλάττοντι should in strict grammar be πλαττούσῃ, to agree with ἡλικίᾳ, but the sense, and the interposition of μειρακίῳ, make πλάττοντι easy to understand.

23 καὶ μέντοι καὶ πάνυ—παρίεμαι - 'Yes, and I particularly beg and entreat this of you.' The first καί = 'and'; the second emphasises πάνυ.

27 ἐπὶ τῶν τραπεζῶν - 'at the bankers' tables'. These tables or counters were set up in the market-place at Athens and were centres of popular resort. ἵνα here = 'where'. The word is not often found in this sense in Attic prose.

[17 D] 28 μήτε θαυμάζειν μήτε θορυβεῖν depend on δέομαι καὶ παρίεμαι, l. 25. 'I beg you not to be surprised, and not to interrupt me.'

30 ἀναβέβηκα - A technical term for appearing before a law-court: ἀνα-βέβηκα, 'I have gone up', probably refers to mounting the platform from which the accuser and accused spoke.

31 τῆς ἐνθάδε λέξεως - 'The style of this place', sc. law-court or forensic oratory. In Greek an adverb is often used between the article and noun instead of an adjective or adjectival phrase. ὁ τότε τύραννος = 'the ruler of that day'. So occasionally in English we find 'the then ruler'.

32 ἄν—ἄν - The ἄν which belongs to ξυνεγιγνώσκετε is doubled, so that the conditional force may be felt through the whole sentence. Sometimes ἄν is thus used three times with the same verb.

33 φωνῇ = 'dialect'.

[18 A] 34 καὶ δὴ καὶ νῦν = 'so as it is'.

35 δίκαιον is in an emphatic position: 'I make this request of you, and it is a just one.'

37 σκοπεῖν depends on δέομαι: see l. 28 above.

38 δικαστοῦ—ἀρετή - 'The excellence of a judge lies in this', lit. 'this is the virtue of a judge'. ἀρετή is predicate. αὕτη is used instead of τοῦτο, by attraction to the gender of ἀρετή. Cf. Virg. *Aen.* VI. 129 *hic labor est.*

CHAPTER II

1 δίκαιός εἰμι ἀπολογήσασθαι - 'It is right that I should defend myself'. Greek idom says 'I am just (δίκαιός εἰμι) to do it', where English says 'it is just (δίκαιόν ἐστι) that I should do it'.

2 ψεύδη - a noun, lit. 'the first falsehoods brought in accusation against me'. μου is governed by κατά in κατηγορημένα.

[18B] 5 καὶ πάλαι - 'even of old.' The next καί is 'and', joining πολλὰ ἤδη ἔτη and οὐδὲν ἀληθὲς λέγοντες: 'talking now for many years and saying nothing true'. Other ways of understanding the construction seem less satisfactory.

7 τοὺς ἀμφὶ Ἄνυτον - 'Anytus and his associates'. Anytus was the most powerful of Socrates' three accusers. See Introduction.

9 ἐκ παίδων - 'in your childhood'.

10 κατηγόρουν—ἀληθές - 'used to accuse me of what is not true'. If μᾶλλον, which is found in the best MS, is kept, it must be taken with κατηγόρουν—'were more busy in accusing me'.

11 τις Σωκράτης - 'one Socrates'. τις shows contempt.
σοφός is ironical, as often in Plato's time.
τά τε μετέωρα φροντιστής - The verbal noun φροντιστής governs the accusative like the verb φροντίζειν. ' One who speculates about the heavens', lit. 'the heavens-speculator'. It would be more natural to have the genitive, and τῶν μετεώρων φροντιστής is actually found in Xenophon. φροντιστής is used contemptuously, like σοφός.

12 τὰ ὑπὸ γῆς—κρείττω ποιῶν - This description refers to the caricature of Socrates in Aristophanes' play, the *Clouds.* Aristophanes mocks at Socrates for having a φροντιστήριον or 'notion-shop'; where the pupils grub in the ground, by way of studying natural science, and are taught to make the worse appear the better cause. λόγος is here 'cause' or 'argument'. ἥττων and κρείττων mean worse and better as regards morality. In the *Clouds* the Just and Unjust Cause have a contest and the Unjust wins.

13 **οὗτοι—οἱ δενοί εἰσίν μου κατήγοροι** - 'These are my dangerous accusers.' The article used in the predicate implies that the dangerous accusers have been mentioned before, and the reference is to δεινότεροι, l. 8.

[18c] 16 **οὐδὲ θεοὺς νομίζειν** - 'Do not believe in gods either'.

18 **ἔτι δὲ καί** - 'and further too'.

19 **ἐν ᾗ ἂν μάλιστα ἐπιστεύσατε** - Williamson seems right in explaining ἐπιστεύσατε ἄν as = ἐμέλλετε πιστεύειν, 'you were likely to believe'.

21 **ἐρήμην** - Supply δίκην. Tr. 'being literally (ἀτεχνῶς) prosecutors in a suit given by default', i.e. where the defendant loses his case, owing to his failure to appear.
ὃ δὲ π. ἄλογ. - To complete the construction τοῦτ' ἔστιν must be supplied.

[18D] 23 **κωμῳδοποιός** - Aristophanes principally, but other comic poets had satirised Socrates.

25 **οἱ δὲ καὶ αὐτοὶ πεπεισμένοι** - These people are a section of the whole class ὅσοι δὲ—χρώμενοι. Tr. 'and some it may be because they have been themselves convinced'.

27 **ἀναβιβάσασθαι** is the causal verb corresponding to ἀναβαίνειν in 17D above, and in the middle voice it = 'to call forward in court on one's behalf'.

30 **ἀξιώσατε** is here 'believe', more often 'think it right'.

[18E] 33 **ἐκείνους** - sc. τοὺς πάλαι, the earlier in point of time, not (as usually) in point of position in the sentence.

[19A] 38 **ἔσχετε** - 'acquired'. The aorist ἔσχετε is to be distinguished from the impf. εἴχετε, which would mean 'had', 'entertained'.

40 **εἴ τι ἄμεινον** - 'if it is in any way better'. τι is adverbial.

41 **πλέον ποιῆσαι** = 'be successful'.

42 **οὐ πάνυ** - As in English 'not exactly pleasant' means 'very far from pleasant', so in Greek οὐ πάνυ με λανθάνει (lit. 'does not altogether escape me') = 'I am far from being unaware', or, 'I am very well aware'.

CHAPTER III

2 **ἡ ἐμὴ διαβολή** - 'the prejudice against me'.

[19B] 3 **Μέλητός με ἐγράψατο τὴν γραφὴν ταύτην** - 'Meletus drew up this indictment against me'. Meletus was nominally the chief accuser of Socrates, but his supporter, Anytus, was a more influential man.

4 ὥσπερ οὖν—αὐτῶν - 'Well I must read their affidavit as it were and take them for formal accusers'. ὥσπερ belongs both to κατηγόρων and to ἀναγνῶναι. At the proceedings preliminary to a trial both parties gave in to the presiding magistrate a written declaration of their case, and swore to the truth of it. The technical term for this affidavit was ἀντωμοσία.

6 περιεργάζεται - 'makes himself a nuisance'; lit. 'does too much'.

[19C] 10 κωμῳδίᾳ. In the *Clouds*.

περιφερόμενον - 'Swinging about'. Socrates in the *Clouds* appears suspended in a wicker-basket. When asked what he is doing he says (225) ἀεροβατῶ καὶ περιφρονῶ (think about) the sun.

12 πέρι governs ὧν. The accent of περί is thrown back according to the custom when a preposition follows its case.

14 μή πως—φύγοιμι - 'I hope I may not be prosecuted on so many charges by Meletus'. φυγεῖν, 'to be defendant in a case', is opposed to διώκειν, 'to be plaintiff'.

15 ἀλλὰ γάρ - 'But really'.

[19D] 20 οἱ τοιοῦτοι - sc. my hearers.

23 περὶ ἐμοῦ would be put by English idiom in the relative clause. 'What most people say about me.'

CHAPTER IV

1 οὔτε—οὐδέ γ' instead of οὔτε—οὔτε, because a special emphasis is thrown upon the second clause.

[19E] 3 ἐπεί - 'although', 'and yet'. This use can be traced from the ordinary meaning 'since' by supplying a clause, e.g. 'I wish it were, since', etc.

5 Γοργίας τε—Ἱππίας ὁ Ἠλεῖος - Gorgias of Leontini in Sicily was a famous teacher of rhetoric. He came to Athens in 427 B.C. on an embassy, and shortly afterwards settled there. Prodicus of the island of Ceos taught grammar and ethics. Hippias of Elis lectured on all the arts and sciences of the day. All these, together with other travelling teachers, were called by the general name of 'sophists', and received what were then considered large fees for their work.

7 οἷός τ' ἐστὶν—βούλωνται - The sentence is not grammatic-

ally complete as it stands. We should expect an infinitive, such as πείθειν or παιδεύειν (educate) οἷός τ᾽ ἐστίν, 'each of them is able to go to every city [and to teach] the young men'. Instead we find τούτους πείθουσι, as if the sentence ran thus: 'they all go to every city...and persuade the young men'.

[20A] 11 **χάριν προσειδέναι** - 'feel gratitude besides', sc. in addition to the fee.

12 **ἐπεί.** See note on ἐπεί 19E above. Here the clause to be supplied is '[And these are not all] since'.

Πάριος - The name of this sophist from the island of Paros is Evenus. It is given below, l. 27.

ὃν ᾐσθόμην - 'who was, I heard'. The acc. after ᾐσθόμην shows that Socrates is speaking from hearsay, and has not met Evenus. In 22C ᾐσθόμην αὐτῶν...οἰομένων, 'I perceived that they thought', the gen. implies personal observation.

15 **Καλλίᾳ** - A very rich Athenian who liked to collect sophists in his house. In the *Protagoras* he appears as the host of several distinguished sophists.

18 **εἴχομεν ἄν** - 'we could have', 'we should have been in a position to'.

19 **ὃς ἔμελλεν** - 'who might have been expected to'. ἔμελλεν is part of the conditional sentence, cf. ἔμελλον (38B) and ἐτεθράμμην (18A).

[20B] 19 **τὴν προσήκουσαν ἀρετήν** - 'in their proper excellence'; the construction is a sort of cognate accusative after the whole expression καλώ τε κἀγαθὼ ποιήσειν.

21 **νῦν δ᾽** - 'but as it is'.

26 **πόσου, πέντε μνῶν** are genitives of price.

29 **ἐμμελῶς** - 'reasonably', lit. 'harmoniously'.

[20C] 31 **ἀλλ᾽ οὐ γὰρ ἐπίσταμαι** - 'but I really do not know'.

CHAPTER V

2 **τὸ σὸν—πρᾶγμα** - τὸ σόν is emphatic, 'what is *your* business?' as opposed to that of the sophists.

4 **ἔπειτα** sums up οὐ γάρ—πραγματευομένου and expresses surprise: 'for surely (δήπου) all these stories and reports have hardly grown up about you while you have been doing nothing more than other people'; lit. 'while you have been doing', etc....'these stories', etc., 'have not then (ἔπειτα) grown up'.

περιττότερον - As in περιεργάζεται 19B, the περι- denotes a doing too much, a meddlesomeness.

5 εἰ μή τι—οἱ πολλοί - 'Unless you *were* doing', not 'unless you *had been* doing'. The clause expresses only a slight variation on the meaning of οὐδέν—πραγματευομένου.

ἀλλοῖον is 'something different', περιττότερον 'something more'.

[20D] 12 ἀλλ' ἤ - 'unless'.

13 ἔσχηκα - have acquired', like ἔσχετε, 'acquired', (19A).

15 ταύτην - cognate acc. after εἶναι σοφός.

[20E] 16 μείζω—σοφίαν - 'a wisdom too great for man', lit. 'a wisdom not according to man's standard', like οὐ κατὰ τούτους εἶναι ῥήτωρ.

17 ἢ οὐκ ἔχω τί λέγω - 'or I know not how to describe it'. λέγω is a deliberative subjunctive.

19 ἐπὶ διαβολῇ τῇ ἐμῇ - 'to raise a prejudice against me'. ἐπί = 'with a view to'. ἐμή = ἐμοῦ, objective genitive, as in ἡ ἐμὴ διαβολή (19A).

21 οὐ γὰρ ἐμὸν—ἀξιόχρεων - ἐμόν and ἀξιόχρεων are both predicates. 'The word that I shall speak is not mine, but the authority to whom I shall refer you is worthy of credit.'

22 τῆς γὰρ—παρέξομαι τὸν θεόν - 'For of my wisdom, if it can be called wisdom, and such as it is, I will call the god as witness'.

24 Χαιρεφῶντα - A friend of Socrates. As Chaerephon was dead ἴστε means 'know about', 'remember'. γάρ, as often, introducing a story, can be left untranslated. The nearest equivalents are 'now', 'well'. See also γάρ below, l. 30.

[21A] 25 τῷ πλήθει - 'your democratic party'. Hardly any of Socrates' disciples were on this side in politics.

26 τὴν φυγὴν ταύτην - 'your recent exile'. In 404 B.C., during the tyranny of the Thirty, 1,500 Athenians were put to death, and more than 5,000 went into exile. Next year the exiles returned with Thrasybulus as their leader. κατέρχεσθαι is the regular word for 'to return from exile'.

28 καὶ δή—καί - 'so once'. καὶ δὴ καί introduces an instance of his being vehement (σφοδρός).

29 τοῦτο refers forward to Chaerephon's question; 'the following enquiry'.

31 ἀνεῖλεν is a technical word used for the answer of an oracle. ἡ Πυθία was the Pythian priestess, who acted as Apollo's mouthpiece at Delphi.

64

CHAPTER VI

[21 B] 1 **μέλλω γάρ** introduces the explanation of *ὧν ἕνεκα*. *γάρ* should not be translated.

4 **οὔτε μέγα οὔτε σμικρόν** - adverbial, 'neither much nor little', i.e. 'not at all'.

5 **σοφὸς ὤν** might have been *σοφῷ ὄντι*, as in 22 C. 'I am aware that I am not at all wise', lit. 'I am conscious to myself'.

[21 C] 11 **τὸ μαντεῖον** - 'the oracle'. *τῷ χρησμῷ*, 'the response', which in the words *σὺ δ' ἐμὲ ἔφησθα* is addressed as a person.

14 **πρὸς ὅν** goes with *ἔπαθον*.

16 **ἔδοξέ μοι** is put ungrammatically but naturally instead of some word like *ἔγνων*, 'I observed'. So in English 'talking with him, he seemed' is often incorrectly said instead of 'talking with him, we thought him'.

[21 D] 19 **ἐντεῦθεν** - 'by so doing'.

21 **ὅτι** introduces Socrates' thought as a direct quotation. 'I thought to myself "I am wiser than this man"' (Church).

23 **καλὸν κἀγαθόν** - used by Socrates for moral excellence, but politically the oligarchical party were called *καλοὶ κἀγαθοί*. Very probably Socrates' habitual use of the expression aggravated the suspicion that he favoured the oligarchical party and so contributed indirectly to his death.

24 **ὥσπερ οὖν** - 'as in point of fact'.

26 **ἃ μὴ οἶδα** - *μή* is used, not *οὐ*, because Socrates is talking of the whole class of things he does not know, not of certain definite things.

CHAPTER VII

21 E] 2 **ὅτι ἀπηχθανόμην** is to be taken with *αἰσθανόμενος*: 'perceiving both with pain and apprehension that I was making enemies'. Some editors leave out *καί* before *λυπούμενος*, thereby making it easier to see that *λυπ.* and *δεδιώς* are subordinate to *αἰσθανόμενος*.

3 **ὅμως δὲ—ἐδόκει** - After *αἰσθανόμενος μέν* we should expect *ὅμως δέ* to be followed by another participle: 'but nevertheless thinking it necessary'. We have, however, the finite verb *ἐδόκει*: 'but nevertheless it seemed necessary'.

4 **ἰτέον οὖν σκοποῦντι** - Supply *μοι*. *ἰτέον μοι* = Lat. *eundum est mihi*. 'So I must go and investigate (lit. investigating) the response'.

6 **νὴ τὸν κύνα** - Socrates used to swear by the dog, the goose and the plane-tree. Also (24E) we find *νὴ τὴν "Ηραν*.

[22A] 7 **οἱ μὲν μάλιστα** - There is no conjunction to join these words to the preceding sentence. *τοιοῦτον* is explained by what follows, and in such a case the conjunction is often omitted.

9 **κατὰ τὸν θεόν** - 'as the god commanded'.

10 **ἐπιεικέστεροι—ἔχειν** - 'to be better fitted for knowledge'. Common people were more conscious of their ignorance, and so more nearly wise.

11 **τὴν ἐμὴν πλάνην** = *τὴν πλάνην μου*, and *πονοῦντος* agrees with the implied *μου*: 'my wandering, like that of one toiling in great labours'. The allusion is to the labours of Hercules.

12 **ἵνα—γένοιτο** - 'that my oracle might be made absolutely (*καί*) irrefutable'. *ἵνα* depends on *πονοῦντος*.

13 **γάρ** here again = 'well'.

15 **διθυράμβων** - The dithyramb was a hymn in honour of Dionysus, sung to the accompaniment of the flute, while the singers danced.

[22B] 15 **ἐπ' αὐτοφώρῳ** - 'red-handed'. Socrates looks on his ignorance as a crime.

18 **πεπραγματεῦσθαι** - passive. **διηρώτων ἄν** - 'I would ask'. This is a common use of the imperf. with *ἄν* to denote actions frequently repeated.

21 **ὡς—ἅπαντες** - 'pretty nearly all'. *ὡς—εἰπεῖν* qualifies *ὀλίγου ἅπαντες*. *αὐτῶν* depends on *βέλτιον*.

22 **οἱ παρόντες** - 'the bystanders'. **αὐτοί** sc. *οἱ ποιηταί*. **ἂν ἔλεγον**, 'would be likely to speak'; past potential use like *ἐπιστεύσατε ἄν* (18C).

23 **ἐν ὀλίγῳ** - supply *χρόνῳ*.

[22C] 24 **ποιοῖεν** - 'wrote poetry'. A poet is a 'maker'.

25 **φύσει—ἐνθουσιάζοντες** - 'by a sort of instinct and inspiration'. To Plato a poet was a person not in control of his wits, but possessed (*κατεχόμενος*) and inspired by the god (*ἔνθεος*, a word from which *ἐνθουσιάζω* is derived).

26 **καὶ γὰρ οὗτοι** - *καί* goes with *οὗτοι*.

30 **ἀνθρώπων** depends on *σοφωτάτων*. 'I perceived that they thought themselves the wisest of men in other respects also, in which they were not wise.'

CHAPTER VIII

2 ἐμαυτῷ —ξυνῄδη - See above on σοφὸς ὤν (21 B).

[22D] 3 τούτους δέ γ' - γε emphasises τούτους.

3 εὑρήσοιμι represents the εὑρήσω of direct speech, according to the regular usage of the fut. opt.

7 ὅπερ—δημιουργοί - 'The good craftsmen also seemed to me to make just the same mistake as the poets'. καί—καί shows the symmetrical balance of the poets and artisans.

8 διὰ τὸ—ἠξίου - An explanatory clause without an introductory conjunction, like οἱ μὲν μάλιστα κτλ. (22 A).

9 τὰ μέγιστα - i.e. politics.

[22 E] 11 ὑπέρ - 'on behalf of'.

13 μήτε τι - 'not at all'. μήτε is put instead of οὔτε because μήτε—ἀμαθίαν goes with the inf. ἔχειν, which naturally takes μή.

14 ἀμφότερα - namely their wisdom and their ignorance.

CHAPTER IX

[23A] 3 οἷαι χαλεπώταται - Supply ἂν εἶεν.

4 ὄνομα δὲ—λέγεσθαι - We should expect ὄνομα δὲ λέγομαι to balance πολλαὶ μέν—γεγόνασι, but the δέ clause has been made to follow ὥστε, and πολλαὶ μέν has no formal antithesis. ὄνομα may be adverbial, 'by name', so that ὄνομα λέγεσθαι = ὀνομάζεσθαι, 'to be called': perhaps, however, it is better to regard ὄνομα as a predicate of τοῦτο, lit. 'so that I am called this as a name'. We sometimes find the pronoun οὗτος joined to a noun in prose without the article, when the noun is used as a predicate; Her. I. 120 δίκην ταύτην ἐπέθηκε, 'he imposed this as a punishment'. In either case τοῦτο refers forward to σοφός.

5 σοφὸς εἶναι - σοφόν in the acc. might be expected. σοφός can be explained because, though the grammatical subject of the whole sentence is πολλαὶ ἀπέχθειαι, the real subject is ἐγώ. εἶναι is redundant. Such an εἶναι is often found after verbs meaning 'to name'. Tr. 'many enmities of a most bitter and grievous kind have been incurred by me, so that much prejudice has arisen from them, and for a title this is what I am called, "a wise man"'. σοφὸς ἀνήρ was a current term of mockery; see on 18 B.

67

6 **αὐτόν** - 'myself'.

τὸ δὲ—τῷ ὄντι - 'whereas in very truth'. In Plato τὸ δέ is often used adverbially, meaning 'but actually'. τῷ ὄντι = 'in reality' strengthens the phrase.

9 **ὀλίγου τινὸς—καὶ οὐδενός** - 'little *or* nothing'. καί corrects ὀλίγου and introduces a stronger word.

φαίνεται—τὸν Σωκράτη κτλ. - 'he appears not to say this' (sc. τὸ σοφὸν εἶναι) 'of Socrates, but to have used my name therein' (πρός—sc. for the purposes of the oracle), 'because he took me as an example'. Socrates means that, in the opinion of the god, the best human wisdom is merely a confession of ignorance.

[23B] 11 **ὥσπερ ἂν εἰ** - sc. ἐμὲ παράδειγμα ποιοῖτο, 'would make me an example, if he were to say'. But ὥσπερ ἂν εἰ comes to mean 'just as if', without consciousness of any ellipse.

12 **ὅτι** is not to be translated. It serves the purpose of quotation marks in Greek. See on ὅτι (21 D).

14 **ταῦτ' οὖν** - ταῦτα often = διὰ ταῦτα, 'for this reason', in Plato and Aristophanes.

17 **τῷ θεῷ βοηθῶν** - 'helping the god' by showing that Socrates, knowing his lack of wisdom, is less unwise than other people.

[23 C] 20 **πενίᾳ μυρίᾳ** - 'infinite poverty'. μύριος is used for any large quantity. We learn from Xenophon that Socrates' total property amounted to about £20.

CHAPTER X

2 **οἱ τῶν πλουσιωτάτων** - sc. the sons of the richest men.

αὐτόματοι - with ἐπακολουθοῦντες.

4 **εἶτα ἐπιχειροῦσιν** - 'and go and try to'. εἶτα introduces the explanation of the way in which Socrates' followers imitate him. It contains in itself the notion of a connecting particle, though we also find κᾆτα = καὶ εἶτα used in the same way as εἶτα alone.

[23 D] 9 **ἀλλ' οὐχ αὐτοῖς** - 'instead of with themselves'.

Σωκράτης τίς ἐστι μιαρώτατος - 'one Socrates is an abominable fellow'.

11 **ὅ τι ποιῶν** - sc. διαφθείρει τοὺς νέους.

13 **τὰ κατὰ—ταῦτα** - 'your ready-made charges against all who study philosophy'. ταῦτα is contemptuous, like *ista* in Latin.

14 ὅτι - sc .διαφθείρει διδάσκων. τά—ὑπὸ γῆς, and also νομίζειν and ποιεῖν depend on διδάσκων.

[23F] 19 ξυντεταγμένως - 'in a studied manner', lit. 'in set array'.

22 ἐκ τούτων - 'of these'. τούτων is masc.

24 Λύκων - We know nothing of Lycon except that he was the mouthpiece of the professional rhetoricians. Anytus was a tanner by profession.

[24A] 26 ὑμῶν—ἐξελέσθαι - 'to rid your minds of'.

28 οὕτω πολλὴν γεγονυῖαν - 'when it has grown so strong'.

ταῦτ᾽ ἔστιν ὑμῖν τἀληθῆ - 'here you have the truth', lit. 'here is the truth for you'.

29 καὶ ὑμᾶς ὑποστειλάμενος - 'and I speak without concealing or suppressing anything from you whatever'. οὔτε μέγα οὔτε μικρόν - 'anything whatever'.

31 οἶδα σχεδόν - 'I know pretty well', i.e. very well.

τοῖς αὐτοῖς - neuter: 'for the same', i.e. for saying this.

[24B] 34 οὕτως εὑρήσετε - sc. ἔχοντα: 'you will find that they are so'.

xI–xV. *Socrates' reply to the indictment of Meletus*

CHAPTER XI

1 ὧν = τούτων ὧν for τούτων ἅ by attraction. See on τῶν πολλῶν ὧν (17A).

5 αὖθις—λάβωμεν - 'let us consider their affidavit in turn', as we did that of the πρῶτοι κατήγοροι from 19B up to this point. γάρ is introductory.

ὥσπερ—κατηγόρων - 'as if these were a new set of accusers'.

7 ἔχει δέ πως ὧδε - 'it runs something like this'. Socrates makes no claim to strict accuracy.

φησίν - sc. Meletus.

[24C] 11 φησὶ γὰρ δή - 'well then, he says'. με is subject to ἀδικεῖν, and τοὺς νέους is governed by διαφθείροντα.

12 ἐγὼ δέ γε - γε emphasises ἐγώ: so also τούτους δέ γ' (22D).

13 ὅτι—χαριεντίζεται - 'because he makes fun in earnest'. What is sport to Meletus is death to Socrates.

16 **ὦν οὐδέν** - ὦν goes with ἐμέλησεν, οὐδέν is adverbial: 'matters which have never been at all of interest to him'.
ἐμέλησεν very likely plays on the name Meletus. So μεμέληκεν (24 D), and ἀμέλειαν (25 C).

CHAPTER XII

1 **καί—εἰπέ** - 'now come, tell me'. καί is common before imperatives, and gives briskness to the exhortation. **δεῦρο,** 'hither' = ἴθι, l. 3.
ἄλλο τι ἤ—ποιεῖ - lit. 'is anything else the case or do you value?' But by Plato's time the phrase ἄλλο τι ἤ, or even ἄλλο τι alone, had become merely an interrogative particle, expecting an affirmative answer, Lat. *nonne?*

[24D] 4 **μέλον γέ σοι** - 'as you take an interest', lit. 'it being a care to you'. The participle of a few verbs used impersonally, most of them compounds of εἶναι, 'to be', e.g. ἐξόν, παρόν, is found in the acc. absolute instead of the genitive.

5 **ἐμέ** belongs to τὸν διαφθείροντα, but is separated for emphasis: 'for having found their corrupter, myself as you say, you are bringing him to trial before these men, and accusing him'.

[24E] 12 **ὅστις—τοὺς νόμους** - 'who starts with a knowledge of just this very thing, the laws'. καί emphasises αὐτὸ τοῦτο.

13 **οὗτοι—οἱ δικασταί** - 'these, Socrates, the jurymen'. οὗτοι points out the jury, and οἱ δικασταί is in apposition, explaining οὗτοι.

18 **τί δὲ δή** - 'what then?' 'again': used to mark a fresh point. **ἀκροαταί** - 'the audience'. Sometimes the number of the public present at trials was large. We hear of visitors from all parts of Greece coming to listen to the famous suit against Ctesiphon for proposing to present a golden crown to Demosthenes.

[25A] 20 **ἀλλ' ἄρα—μή** expects the answer 'no'.

25 **πολλήν—δυστυχίαν** - καταγιγνώσκειν here means 'to espy a weak spot in a man': the person is put in the genitive, and the weakness, in this case πολλὴν δυστυχίαν, in the accusative, 'you have made me out to be very unfortunate'. Judicially καταγιγνώσκειν = 'to condemn'.

[25B] 27 **οἱ μὲν βελτίους** - sc. δοκοῦσι. There is no conjunction because οἱ μὲν βελτίους explains οὕτω; see on οἱ μὲν μάλιστα (22A).

29 **τοὐναντίον—πᾶν** - These words are in apposition to the whole sentence. Similarly in English we might say: 'he upset the milk-jug—an awkward blunder'.

33 **ἐάν τε—οὐ φῆτε** - οὐ φῆτε, 'you deny', is regarded as a single word, and therefore οὐ is retained, though μή is the proper negative to go with εἰ or ἐάν.

34 **πολλὴ γὰρ—διαφθείρει** - 'it would be a great piece of good fortune for our young men, if only one man corrupts them'. The indicative διαφθείρει implies that the words of Meletus are referred to. Grammatically the optative διαφθείροι might have been expected, so as to correspond with ἄν—εἴη, but then there would have been no such reference.

[25 C] 36 **ἀλλὰ γάρ** - See on 19 C.

38 **ἀμέλειαν—μεμέληκεν** - A play on Meletus' name. See on 24 C.

CHAPTER XIII

1 **πρὸς Διός** - 'in Heaven's name', used in entreaties, as contrasted with νὴ Δία and μὰ Δία, the affirmative and negative asseverations.

3 **ὦ τάν** - 'my dear sir'. The derivation of τάν is uncertain: possibly it is connected with τύ = σύ.

5 **ἀεί** - 'from time to time', or 'at any time'.

6 **βούλεται** - The argument is as follows: πονηροί injure (κακὸν ἐργάζονται) their companions. Nobody desires (βούλεται) to be injured. But, if I corrupt the young, I make them πονηροί and therefore, as their companion, am injured. Therefore, if I corrupt the young, I do so unwillingly. The word βούλεται is regularly used by Socrates in reasoning of this kind. It is easy to pick holes in the proof.

[25 D] 8 **καὶ γὰρ—ἀποκρίνεσθαι** - Such a law is quoted in the speech of [Demosthenes] *In Stephanum II*, 10.

12 **σὺ—τηλικόσδε ὤν** - 'are you at your age so much wiser than I at mine?' Meletus was a young man when the trial took place.

13 **ὥστε σὺ μὲν—ἐγὼ δὲ δή** - 'that whereas you know...I forsooth'. δή shows the irony. Greek often makes sentences co-ordinate by means of μέν and δέ, where English would use a subordinate sentence for the μέν clause, e.g. 'though I thought of it, you did it', ἐγὼ μὲν ἐνόησα, σὺ δ' ἔπραξας.

71

[25E] 16 **εἰς τοσοῦτον—ἥκω** - lit. 'I have come to such a point of ignorance', 'I am so sunk in ignorance'.

καὶ τοῦτ' ἀγνοῶ - τοῦτο refers forward to ὅτι—λαβεῖν ἀπ' αὐτοῦ.

18 **ὑπ' αὐτοῦ** - κακὸν λαβεῖν is virtually a passive, and can be followed by ὑπό of the agent, like πεπόνθατε ὑπό (17A). Another reading is ἀπ' αὐτοῦ.

20 **οἶμαι δέ** - sc. πείθεσθαι.

[26A] 22 **ἄκων** - sc. διαφθείρω. **κατ' ἀμφότερα** - 'both ways', 'in either case'.

23 **τῶν τοιούτων καὶ ἀκουσίων** - These words are a genitive of the charge after εἰσάγειν.

25 **ἐὰν μάθω** - 'if I am taught'. μανθάνω often serves as the passive of διδάσκω, as πάσχω is the pass. of ποιῶ in 17A.

παύσομαι - ποιῶν.

29 **ἀλλ' οὐ** - 'and not'. Cf. ἀλλ' οὐχ αὐτοῖς (23D), 'instead of with themselves', or 'and not with themselves'.

CHAPTER XIV

[26B] 5 **ἢ δῆλον δὴ ὅτι** - sc. φής με διαφθείρειν.

7 **οὐ ταῦτα—διδάσκων** - ταῦτα is acc. after διδάσκων; its position is emphatic.

8 **πάνυ μὲν οὖν—λέγω** - 'yes, that is what I do not emphatically mean'. μὲν οὖν is here an affirmative particle, but it often means 'nay rather'.

10 **ὧν νῦν ὁ λόγος ἐστίν** = οὓς νῦν λέγομεν, 'whom we now mention', not 'about whom we are now talking'.

[26C] 12 **πότερον** is answered by ἢ παντάπασί με, l. 16.

εἶναι τινὰς θεούς - 'that there are *some* gods'; if εἶναί τινας be read there is no emphasis on 'some'.

13 **ἄρα** - 'consequently'.

16 **ὅτι ἑτέρους** - sc. διδάσκω νομίζειν.

οὔτε—τε - like *neque—que* in Latin.

19 **ἵνα τί** - 'wherefore'; in full the phrase would be ἵνα τί γένηται, 'in order that what may happen', 'for what purpose?'

[26D] 19 **οὐδὲ ἥλιον οὐδὲ σελήνην** - In the *Symposium* Plato describes Socrates as offering prayers to the sun.

21 **μὰ Δί'** - 'no, by Zeus'.

ὦ ἄνδρες δικασταί - Meletus uses this regular form of addressing the court, whereas Socrates says ὦ ἄνδρες Ἀθηναῖοι, until after the verdict, when he addresses those who voted in his favour by the formula ὦ ἄνδρες δικασταί (40Α).

22 **'Αναξαγόρου—κατηγορεῖν -** 'do you think that you are prosecuting Anaxagoras?' Anaxagoras came to Athens from Clazomenae in Asia Minor about 463 B.C. He was a very original thinker, and was the first man in Greece to declare that Reason governed the universe. Aristotle calls him, in comparison with earlier philosophers, 'a sober man among babblers' (*Met.* I. 984ᵇ. 17). He said that the sun was 'a red-hot mass of stone', larger than the Peloponnesus; the moon was inhabited and had hills and ravines. Pericles and Euripides were his intimate friends, and Socrates was attracted to his philosophy but afterwards gave it up. He left Athens, being accused of impiety.

25 **ὥστε οὐκ εἰδέναι -** ὥστ' οὐκ (instead of μή) is used here with the infinitive, because the words are in *Oratio Obliqua*, dependent on οἴει.

τὰ 'Αναξ. βιβλία - Anaxagoras wrote a book called περὶ φύσεως, 'On Nature', and other works.

26 **καὶ δὴ καί** introduces an ironical climax, 'ay, and the young', etc.

28 **εἰ πάνυ πολλοῦ -** 'at most'.

[26Ε] 28 **ἐκ τῆς ὀρχήστρας -** Probably the orchestra is not here the circular dancing-place in the theatre, but a round terrace called ὀρχήστρα in or near the market-place (ἀγορά). There is ancient evidence that there was a book market in the neighbourhood of the ἀγορά. A drachma—about ten-pence—is an extremely small price for a scientific book in MS., but the cost of other things in ancient Greece seems sometimes astonishingly low to us. The fare for a passenger on a ship from the Black Sea to Athens is said by Plato (*Gorg.* 511D) to have been two drachmae at most, and it is conceivable that Anaxagoras' book might have been occasionally (ἐνίοτε) picked up for half that amount. We know practically nothing of the price of books at Athens, but there are indications in Aristophanes that they could not have been dear.

Another view is that 'buying from the orchestra for a drachma' means paying a drachma for a theatre ticket to hear the doctrines of Anaxagoras sung in the choral odes of the plays of Euripides and others. But, among other objections, there is the serious one that the charge for admission to the theatre never seems to have been anything but two obols, i.e. one-third of a drachma.

30 **ἄλλως τε—ὄντα** - 'especially as they are so absurd'.

31 **οὑτωσί σοι δοκῶ** - 'is *this* what you think of me?' οὑτωσί refers forward to the next question, and is explained by it.

32 **ἄπιστός γ' εἶ** - ἄπιστος is passive, 'no one believes you'.

36 **νεότητι** - 'recklessness of youth'.

ἔοικεν γὰρ—διαπειρωμένῳ - ὥσπερ αἴνιγμα ξυντιθέντι seems to be subordinate to διαπειρωμένῳ, which is governed by ἔοικεν; 'he seems by framing a sort of riddle to be trying me to see if', etc.

[27A] 38 **γνώσεται** - 'perceive', 'guess', with a genitive.

ὁ σοφὸς δή - δή shows σοφός to be ironical.

41 **τὰ ἐναντία—ἑαυτῷ** - 'to contradict himself'.

ὥσπερ ἂν εἰ - See on 23B.

CHAPTER XV

1 **ἧ μοι—λέγειν** - sc. how he contradicts himself.

This chapter seeks to prove the self-contradiction of Meletus. The indictment (24B) says that Socrates believes in δαιμόνια καινά. 'But', says Socrates, 'as man cannot believe in ἱππικά without believing in ἵπποι and so forth, neither can he believe in δαιμόνια without believing in δαίμονες. Now you allow that I believe in δαιμόνια; therefore I believe in δαίμονες.'

Further, δαίμονες are either gods, or children of gods. If they are gods, then you own that I believe in gods; but if children of gods, you cannot have children without parents. Therefore, since I believe in the children of gods, I must believe in gods, but you have just said (26E) that I have no belief whatever in any god.

3 **ὅπερ—παρῃτησάμην** - He begged them at the beginning in 17C not to make interruptions.

[27B] 3 **μέμνησθέ μοι** - 'remember, please'.

4 **ἐν τῷ εἰωθότι τρόπῳ** - sc. by question and answer and everyday instances.

7 **μὴ ἄλλα—θορυβείτω** - 'do not let him keep on interrupting'.

11 **τοῖς ἄλλοις τουτοισί** - sc. the jury and the audience (ἀκροαταί, 24E).

12 τὸ ἐπὶ τούτῳ γε - 'my next question at least'.

[27C] 14 ὡς ὤνησας - 'how kind of you!' lit.'how you have obliged me' (ὤνησας, fr. ὀνίνημι). μόγις, 'though reluctantly'. The reluctance is not part of the kindness.

15 δαιμόνια—νομίζειν - If the argument is to hold good δαιμόνια πράγματα must be identical with δαιμόνια. Here they can be so identified, because, when the indictment says δαιμόνια, the δαιμόνιον of Socrates is meant (for which see Introduction), and that was a 'divine sign', or something belonging to δαίμονες, a δαιμόνιον πρᾶγμα, not an actual δαίμων.

17 ἀλλ' οὖν - 'at all events'.

18 ἀντιγραφῇ - 'deposition', 'affidavit'. Here ἀντιγρ. = ἀντωμοσία (19Β).

[27D] 22 ἤτοι—γε or ἤτοι alone is regularly used with the first of two alternatives, when it is more emphatic than the second.

26 οὐχ ἡγούμενον—ἡγεῖσθαι πάλιν - 'to say that I, while I do not believe in gods, do still believe in gods'. τοῦτο, l. 24, refers forward.

29 λέγονται - sc. παῖδες εἶναι.

[27E] 31 ὥσπερ ἄν - sc. ἄτοπον εἴη.
ἢ καὶ ὄνων - 'or, if you like, asses'. Either ἤ before καί or τοὺς ἡμιόνους must be cut out. If τοὺς ἡμιόνους were kept, ὄνων would correspond with the nymphs, ἵππων with the gods, and ἵππους δὲ καὶ ὄνους μὴ ἡγοῖτο would imply that Socrates was charged with disbelieving in nymphs, but he was not.

33 οὐκ ἔστιν ὅπως—οὐχί - 'it cannot be but that'. ταῦτα refers forward to τὴν γραφὴν ταύτην, 'in this way, namely on this charge, you have indicted me'.

36 ὅπως δὲ σύ—μηχανή ἐστιν - 'but you cannot possibly persuade' (οὐδεμία μηχανή ἐστιν, ὅπως σὺ πείθοις ἄν) 'anyone who has the smallest understanding, that one and the same individual' (ὡς τοῦ αὐτοῦ ἐστιν, lit. 'that it belongs to the same person') 'will not believe in things supernatural and divine and in daemons and gods, or again, that one and the same individual will not disbelieve in things supernatural and divine and in daemons and gods'.

This is the translation of the text as printed. The insertions ⟨καὶ δαίμονας καὶ θεοὺς⟩ and ⟨μήτε δαιμόνια μήτε θεῖα⟩ were made (by Wecklein) as it is difficult to account for the οὐ in

75

ὡς οὐ τοῦ αὐτοῦ without them. μήτε ἥρωας is bracketed, because ἥρωας can only mean those daemons who are sons of gods and nymphs or other mothers, and is superfluous. If Plato wrote μήτε ἥρωας, he would probably have put the words before θεούς.

Mr H. W. Garrod (*Class. Rev.* vol. xx), however, following other scholars, suggests what seems a satisfactory way of translating the text without any insertions, thus: 'it is impossible that you should persuade anyone with a grain of sense that the man who believes in δαιμόνια must not also believe in θεῖα, and again that the man who disbelieves in either deities or gods or heroes must not disbelieve in all three'; i.e. one must believe in both δαιμόνια *and* θεῖα (καί— καί), if one believes in either, and one must disbelieve in δαίμονες *and* θεοί *and* ἥρωες, if one disbelieves in any of the three.

With this view, the reasons for bracketing μήτε ἥρωας remain the same as before.

XVI–XXII. *Socrates defends himself against popular reproaches*

CHAPTER XVI

[28A]   1 ἀλλὰ γάρ - as in 19C and elsewhere.

2 οὐκ ἀδικῶ - 'am not guilty'.

4 ἐν τοῖς ἔμπροσθεν - in ch. IX.

6 καὶ τοῦτ'—ἐάνπερ αἱρῇ - 'this is what will cause my condemnation, if I am condemned', lit. 'what will catch me, if it does catch me'. διαβολή and φθόνος are personified as prosecutors.

8 πολλοὺς—ἄνδρας - 'many other good men too': the first καί is 'too', meaning 'as well as myself'; the second joins πολλούς and ἀγαθούς in the ordinary Greek way, where English leaves out 'and', saying 'many good', not 'many and good'.

9 οὐδὲν δὲ—στῇ - 'there is no danger of their stopping with me'. Socrates will not be the last victim.

[28B]   10 εἶτ' οὐκ αἰσχύνει - 'what, are you not ashamed?' εἶτα and ἔπειτα in a question express surprise. See on ἔπειτα (20C), and cf. εἶτα (23C), where, though there is no question, indignation or surprise is certainly implied.

13 ὅτι introduces a quotation, as frequently.

εἰ οἴει—ἄνδρα - ἄνδρα is the subject of ὑπολογίζεσθαι.

14 τοῦ ζῆν ἢ τεθνάναι - ζῆν ἢ τεθνάναι forms one notion, so that one τοῦ is enough for both infinitives.

15 ὅτου—ὄφελός ἐστιν - 'in whom there is any good at all', lit. 'of whom there is any use'. Colloquial English employs the word 'use' in the same sense as ὄφελος, in such phrases as 'he is no use' (i.e. good for nothing).

[28 c] 18 τῶν ἡμιθέων - i.e. 'of the heroes'. Heroes are called demigods in Hesiod and in Homer.

19 οἵ τε ἄλλοι καί - 'especially', lit. 'the rest and': the phrase leads up to the climax.

ὁ τῆς Θέτιδος υἱός - The reference is to Il. XVIII. 70 ff. Thetis tells Achilles that death awaits him if he avenge the slaying of Patroclus, but he declares that he will do and die, rather than be shamed by leaving his friend unavenged.

20 παρὰ τὸ—ὑπομεῖναι - 'compared with enduring a disgrace', lit. 'alongside of the enduring something disgraceful'. τό goes with ὑπομεῖναι, and αἰσχρόν τι is the object after the infinitive.

22 θεὸς οὖσα - In Attic prose θεός is a goddess as well as a god. As a deity Thetis can prophesy truly.

23 ὦ παῖ—ἀποθανεῖ - In Il. XVIII. 95 Thetis gives the gist of this sentence. The line begins ὠκύμορος δή μοι, τέκος, ἔσσεαι.

25 αὐτίκα—ἑτοῖμος is an almost exact quotation of Il. XVIII. 96, which runs αὐτίκα γάρ τοι ἔπειτα μεθ' Ἕκτορα πότμος ἑτοῖμος. Notice that Socrates' substitution of φησί for ἔπειτα keeps the hexameter rhythm.

26 ὁ δέ - After ὥστε ἐπειδὴ εἶπεν ἡ μήτηρ, l. 21, we should have expected ἐκεῖνος or 'Ἀχιλλεύς without a δέ; ὥστε is not followed by a verb till ὠλιγώρησε, but Thetis has made so long a speech that ὥστε is forgotten; moreover δέ is fairly often used resumptively after a long subordinate clause.

[28 D] 28 τὸ ζῆν κακὸς ὤν - 'to live a coward'. τὸ ζῆν is the object after δείσας, 'fearing a coward's life'.

29 αὐτίκα—ἀρούρης - Socrates gives the substance of Il. XVIII. 98 and 104 αὐτίκα τεθναίην—ἀλλ' ἧμαι (I sit) παρὰ νηυσὶν ἐτώσιον ἄχθος ἀρούρης. For ἐτώσιον, 'useless', Socrates substitutes κορώνισιν, 'crooked'. By saying οὑτωσί πως, l. 23, he informs us that he does not expect to quote exactly.

31 μὴ οἴει - μή expects the answer 'no', as regularly; see 25 A.

36 μηδὲν ὑπολογιζόμενον - 'taking no heed of'.

37 πρὸ τοῦ αἰσχροῦ - 'before disgrace', or 'in comparison with disgrace': fear of shame should be the first thought, death or danger only the second.

CHAPTER XVII

1 ἐγὼ οὖν δεινὰ—λίποιμι τὴν τάξιν - This sentence summarises the whole chapter, which is a development of Socrates' reply to the reproach (28B) that he ought to be ashamed of a vocation which exposes him to the risk of capital punishment. The god has called him to his mode of life; if fear of death caused him to desist from the pursuit of wisdom, he would be a soldier deserting his post. Never has he so disgraced himself, when under the orders of fellow-citizens, much less will he do so when the god is his superior officer.

[28E] 2 εἰ ὅτε μὲν—Δηλίῳ - 'if, when the officers', etc.; τότε μὲν—ἀποθανεῖν - 'I then stood my ground', etc.; τοῦ δὲ θεοῦ τάττοντος—τοὺς ἄλλους - 'but now, when the god', etc.; ἐνταῦθα δὲ—τὴν τάξιν - 'in this case, I were to desert my post through fear of death or anything else'. ὅτε μέν—Δηλίῳ is summed up by τότε μέν, l. 4, and contrasted with τοῦ δὲ θεοῦ—τοὺς ἄλλους, which in its turn is summed up by ἐνταῦθα δέ. εἰ controls ἔμενον in the μέν clause, λίποιμι τὴν τάξιν in the δέ clause. ἔμενον is indicative, because it refers to an actual fact in the past; λίποιμι is optative, because the contingency is future and remote.

οἱ ἄρχοντες - i.e. generals. Ten generals were elected annually by show of hands.

3 ὑμεῖς εἴλεσθε - 'You chose', meaning by 'you' the whole people, ἄνδρες Ἀθηναῖοι, not the jury, ἄνδρες δικασταί.

καὶ ἐν Ποτιδαίᾳ—Δηλίῳ - At the battle of Potidaea, 432 B.C., Callias was general, and Socrates saved the life of Alcibiades; in the campaign before the town of Amphipolis, 422 B.C., Cleon was general and was killed in a battle: we do not know what was the special part of Socrates; after the defeat of the Athenians under Hippocrates at Delium, in 424 B.C., Socrates showed great gallantry in the retreat.

[29A] 10 τἄν = τοι ἄν.

11 ὅτι οὐ νομίζω—οὐκ ὤν - 'for not believing in the existence of gods, if I disobeyed the oracle through fear of death and the

notion that I am wise when I am not'. καὶ δεδιώς—οὐκ ὤν is subordinate in meaning to ἀπειθῶν, though grammatically parallel to it.

15 ἃ οὐκ οἶδεν - sc. τις.

οἶδε—τὸν θάνατον - 'no one knows about death, whether it is not even the greatest of blessings to man'. Death is put as the object of οἶδε, instead of the subject to τυγχάνει. This is a common idiom, when οἶδα is the verb.

[29 B]   18 καὶ τοῦτο—ἐπονείδιστος - 'why, is not this that reprehensible ignorance?' ἐπονείδιστος refers to 21 D ff. αὕτη ἡ shows that the ignorance has been mentioned before.

20 τούτῳ καὶ ἐνταῦθα - 'in this matter here too'.

21 διαφέρω - 'am different from', i.e. 'better than'.

22 τούτῳ ἄν - sc. φαίην σοφώτερος εἶναι.

23 οὕτω καὶ οἴομαι is written as though ὥσπερ οὐκ οἶδα, instead of its equivalent οὐκ εἰδώς, had gone before.

26 πρὸ οὖν τῶν κακῶν - 'before the evils'. See on 28 D πρὸ τοῦ αἰσχροῦ. ὧν is attracted for ἅ, and is the object of οἶδα in the same way as θάνατον, l. 16, where see note.

28 ὥστ' οὐδ' εἰ—εἴποιμ' ἄν - The long protasis is in three sections: (1) εἰ—ἀφίετε, with amplifications down to διαφθαρήσονται; (2) εἰ—εἴποιτε, with the imaginary speech of the jury, ὦ Σώκρατες—ἀποθανεῖ; (3) εἰ—ἀφίοιτε. Then follows the apodosis εἴποιμ' ἄν, with amplifications down to φροντίζεις, l. 49. εἴποιτε in (2) is a less vivid verb than ἀφίετε, and is therefore put in the optative; and when the verb ἀφιέναι is repeated in (3) it is found in the optative by a sort of attraction to εἴποιτε.

[29 C]   29 τὴν ἀρχήν or ἀρχήν = 'at all', in negative clauses.

30 εἰσελθεῖν - sc. as defendant.

οὐχ—τὸ μὴ ἀποκτεῖναι - 'that it was impossible to refrain from putting me to death', lit. 'that the not-putting-me-to-death was impossible'. It would be more usual to have τὸ μὴ οὔ, but τὸ μή with the infinitive is also sometimes found in negative sentences expressing impossibility.

31 εἰ διαφευξοίμην - Future optative, used correctly to represent in indirect speech the εἰ διαφεύξεται that Anytus would have used.

32 ἄν—διαφθαρήσονται - ἄν appears occasionally to be used with the future indicative in Attic Greek, after allowing for many cases that can be explained through MS. errors.

[29D]   38 **εἰ οὖν -** οὖν sums up the long protasis like *igitur* in Latin.

41 **οὐ μὴ παύσωμαι -** 'I will certainly not cease'. οὐ μή is used with the aorist subjunctive to express a very strong denial.

43 **ὅτῳ ἄν—ὑμῶν** is in apposition to ὑμῖν, 'whomsoever of you I meet from time to time'.

45 **εὐδοκιμωτάτης εἰς σοφίαν καὶ ἰσχύν -** 'most renowned for wisdom and strength'. εἰς = 'in respect of'. ἰσχύς here means strength of character as well as physical power.

46 **χρημάτων μὲν—ἐπιμελούμενος** would strictly be balanced if φρονήσεως δὲ—οὐκ αἰσχύνει οὐκ ἐπιμελούμενος οὐδὲ φροντί- ζων were written, 'while you are not ashamed that you do not care for wisdom or think about her'. In place of this, however, Plato makes a lively transition to 'while you care not'.

[29E]   51 **ἐρήσομαι—ἐξετάσω—ἐλέγξω -** 'I will question, cross-question and test'. The words mark three successive stages in the Socratic method.

[30A]   55 **νεωτέρῳ—ποιήσω -** 'I will do this to whomsoever I meet, whether young or old'. The datives (instead of accusatives) mark that the process is for the good of those questioned.

[30B]   63 **μηδέ** joins πρότερον and οὕτω σφόδρα - Tr. 'before or so earnestly as'.

64 **οὐκ ἐκ χρημάτων -** The omission of ὅτι after λέγων heightens the solemnity of Socrates' declaration.

66 **εἰ—διαφθείρω -** a reference to the words of Meletus as in 25B, where see note.

68 **οὐδὲν λέγει -** 'he is wrong', lit. 'he says nothing'. So λέγει τι means 'he is right'.

πρὸς ταῦτα - 'therefore'.

70 **ὡς ἐμοῦ—ἄλλα -** ὡς is often used with the genitive absolute after an imperative.

ἂν ποιήσοντος - ἄν is occasionally found with the fut. participle as with the fut. indicative; see on ἂν—δαφθαρή- σονται, l. 32 above.

[30C]   71 **τεθνάναι -** strictly 'be dead' is more emphatic than ἀποθνήσκειν which might be expected.

CHAPTER XVIII

2 **οἷς ἐδεήθην ὑμῶν** - in 17D and 20E.

6 **εὖ γὰρ ἴστε** - γάρ is introductory, as we have often had it in this speech. Socrates begins with the recitation of the statements with which he expects to startle his audience.

[30D] 12 **καὶ ἄλλος τις** - 'and many another'.

[30E] 21 **εἰ καὶ γελοιότερον εἰπεῖν** - supply ἐστί.

20 **προσκείμενον** - 'granted', lit. 'added'. προσκεῖσθαι is used as the passive of προστεθεικέναι. Cf. the use of πάσχειν as the passive of ποιεῖν (17A).

22 **νωθεστέρῳ** - 'somewhat sluggish'; a common use of the comparative.

23 **μύωπός τινος** - 'a sort of gad-fly'.
οἷον δή—τινα - 'even as such one the god seems to have granted me to the city—a person who'. οἷον refers to μύωπός τινος, τοιοῦτόν τινα forwards to ὅς—παύομαι.

25 **οὐδὲν παύομαι—προσκαθίζων** - 'never cease from settling upon you at every point the whole day long'.

[31A] 29 **τάχ' ἂν—ἂν—ἂν** - ἄν belongs in each case to ἀποκτείναιτε. For the repetition of ἄν see note on 17D.
ὥσπερ—ἐγειρόμενοι - 'like those aroused from sleep' (lit. when sleeping), or 'like sleepers awakened', according to whether we take οἱ with ἐγειρόμενοι or with νυστάζοντες; perhaps the former is best.

30 **κρούσαντες** - 'crushing', i.e. like a man squashing a mosquito with his hand. The δῆμος is now a drowsy man, not a drowsy horse as in 30E above.

31 **εἶτα—διατελοῖτε ἂν** - 'and you will go and continue': see on εἶτα (23C).

34 **τοιοῦτος οἷος—δεδόσθαι** - 'the sort of man to have been given'.

[31B] 35 **οὐ γὰρ—ἔοικε** - 'it does not seem like human nature', lit. 'it is not like a human thing'. γάρ is introductory. The subject to ἔοικε is τὸ ἐμὲ—ἠμεληκέναι, 'that I should have neglected', 'my neglect'.

36 **ἀνέχεσθαι—ἀμελουμένων** - 'that I should endure [to see] my own affairs being neglected'. ἀνέχεσθαι takes the acc. or the gen. with or without a participle.

37 **τὸ δὲ—πράττειν** - 'that I should act in your interest'.

41 **εἶχον—λόγον** - 'there would have been some sense in

me', i.e. 'I should have seemed reasonable' (lit. 'had reason').

43 **τοῦτό γε—ἀπαναισχυντῆσαι** - 'were not able to contend unblushingly'. τοῦτό γε refers forward to ὡς ἐγὼ—ᾖτησα.

[31 C] 46 **ἱκανὸν—τὴν πενίαν** - ἱκανόν is a predicate, 'the witness that I bring forward of the truth of my words is enough—my poverty'.

CHAPTER XIX

3 **οὐ τολμῶ—πλῆθος** - 'I do not dare to come forward before the people'. ἀναβαίνειν probably means 'to mount the speakers' platform' in the assembly: see on ἀναβέβηκα (17 D).

[31 D] 6 **θεῖόν τι καὶ δαιμόνιον** - 'something divine and supernatural'. For Socrates' δαιμόνιον see Introduction. φωνή is probably added by some ancient note-writer.

ὃ—ἐγράψατο - 'which as you know (δή) is just what Meletus jestingly set down in his indictment'. Socrates refers to the words of the indictment ἕτερα δαιμόνια καινά (24 C).

7 **ἐμοὶ δὲ—ἀρξάμενον** - 'this has been with me ever since my childhood', lit. 'beginning from childhood'.

8 **γιγνομένη** - 'coming to me'.

9 **τοῦτο—πράττειν** - 'turns me from doing that which I am about to do'. τοῦτο is object to πράττειν.

13 **πάλαι—πάλαι** - The repetition implies that Socrates' political career would have been soon ended by his death at the hands of the people.

[31 E] 17 **πλήθει** - 'democratic community'.

[32 A] 20 **τῷ ὄντι** - 'in reality'. **καὶ εἰ**, 'even if'.

CHAPTER XX

3 **οὐδ᾽ ἂν ἑνί** - 'not to anyone in the world', is more emphatic than οὐδενὶ ἄν.

4 **παρὰ—θάνατον** - 'contrary to the right, through fear of death'.

μὴ ὑπείκων—ἀπολοίμην - If the text is right, the first ἅμα goes with ὑπείκων, the second with ἀπολοίμην. Tr. 'and that at one and the same moment I would refuse to yield and also would perish'; i.e. 'I would perish on the spot sooner than give way'. The expression is unusual, and many attempts have been made to emend it.

6 **φορτικὰ μὲν καὶ δικανικά** - 'arrogant clap-trap of the law-courts'. φορτικά (connected with φόρτος, a burden) means what is boring and in bad taste, e.g., here, self-praise. δικανικά means the sort of thing commonly heard in law-courts.

[32B] 8 **ἡμῶν ἡ φυλὴ Ἀντιοχίς** - 'our tribe, Antiochis'.

9 **πρυτανεύουσα** - The Athenian Council (βουλή) of 500 contained 50 members from each of the 10 tribes. Each of these sets of 50 served for the tenth part of a year (πρυτανεία = 35 or 36 days), and the members serving were called Prytanes (πρυτάνεις). A president (ἐπιστάτης τῶν πρυτάνεων) was chosen by lot every day to hold office for a day and a night, who kept the State keys and seal, and presided at meetings of the Assembly (ἐκκλησία) and Council. The chief business of the Council was to receive foreign envoys, take cognisance of serious offences, prepare the business for the Assembly, and maintain order at its meetings.

τοὺς δέκα στρατηγοὺς - At the naval battle of Arginusae, 406 B.C., near the end of the Peloponnesian War, the Athenians defeated the Spartans. Many Athenian sailors were left to drown, when their ships sank after the battle, and no effort was made to recover their bodies. Whether this happened on account of bad weather or through a misunderstanding is not clear. Six of the ten Athenian generals were thereupon tried and executed. Two refused to obey the order of recall, and two were not present at the battle. Plato's use of the word 'ten' is not accurate. Ten was the full number of generals.

10 **ἀνελομένους** is regularly used of taking up dead bodies after a battle.

11 **παρανόμως—ἔδοξε** - At the trial it was proposed that the generals should be condemned or acquitted in a body (ἄθροοι). This was contrary to a statute which declared it illegal to vote upon the case of two or more accused persons at once.

11 **ἐν τῷ ὑστέρῳ χρόνῳ** - Xenophon says that the Athenians in wrath allowed the proposer, Callixenus, to starve to death.

12 **ἐγώ—ἐψηφισάμην** - Probably this refers to the attitude of Socrates at a meeting of the πρυτάνεις to discuss the proposal of Callixenus, before the question was put in the Assembly. Xenophon tells us that other prytanes objected at first to the

proposal of Callixenus, but withdrew their opposition in fear of the angry multitude.

14 **ἐνδεικνύναι με καὶ ἀπάγειν** - 'to indict and arrest me'. *ἐνδεικνύναι*, as a legal term, is to give information to the magistrate of a person who is wrongly exercising a privilege, and call for the offender's summary arrest and punishment: *ἀπάγειν* is to arrest a wrong-doer red-handed. The mob held that the resistance of Socrates was a punishable offence.

[32c] 18 **δεσμόν** - 'imprisonment'.

20 **οἱ τριάκοντα** - 'the Thirty', in later times called 'the Thirty Tyrants'. After the Peloponnesian War an oligarchy of thirty was established at Athens, with the co-operation of the victorious Spartan general. The tyranny of this government soon produced a democratic reaction.

21 **πέμπτον αὐτόν** - 'with four others', lit. 'myself the fifth'. Phrases of this kind generally indicate that the person named is the principal member of the company. A general who is *δέκατος αὐτός* is a general with full powers, as there were ten generals in all.

θόλον - A Rotunda (or *Σκιάς*, 'parasol', so called from its shape) where the prytanes dined, and also the Thirty, while they were in power.

22 **Λέοντα** - Xenophon, *Hell.* II. 3. 39, tells us that he was a well-known and innocent inhabitant of Salamis.

23 **ἀποθάνοι** - 'be put to death': *ἀποθανεῖν* is used as the passive of *ἀποκτείνειν*; see on *πεπόνθατε* (17A).

οἷα δή is governed by *προσέταττον*.

24 **ἀναπλῆσαι** - 'to implicate in', lit. 'to fill up with', takes a genitive.

[32D] 26 **εἰ μὴ—εἰπεῖν** - 'if the expression is not too blunt'. In full the sentence would run: 'I would say' (*ἔλεγον ἄν*) 'if the expression were not, etc.' Socrates thinks *οὐδ' ὁτιοῦν μέλει*, 'I do not care a straw', needs some toning down.

28 **τούτου δέ** sums up the whole clause *τοῦ δέ—ἐργάζεσθαι*.

29 **ἐκείνη ἡ ἀρχή** - sc. the Thirty. Their rule lasted 8 months.

30 **ὥστε** is to be taken after *ἐξέπληξεν*, not with *οὕτως ἰσχυρά*. Tr. 'did not terrify me into doing anything wrong, though it' (sc. the government) 'was so powerful'.

CHAPTER XXI

[32 E] 3 τοῖς δικαίοις - neuter: the plural refers to repeated occasions, 'I maintained the right in every case'.

5 οὐδὲ γὰρ—οὐδείς - 'no, nor would anybody else': supply διεγένετο.

[33 A] 7 τοιοῦτος φανοῦμαι - 'I shall be found to be like this', implies ἐάν με ἐξετάσητε, 'if you examine me', or the like, to complete the sense. τοιοῦτος refers forward to οὐδενὶ—ξυγχωρήσας.

ἰδίᾳ ὁ αὐτὸς οὗτος - 'and in my private life just the same': supply φανοῦμαι.

12 τὰ ἐμαυτοῦ πράττοντος - 'fulfilling my mission'.

13 ἐφθόνησα is attracted to the aorist ἐγενόμην: we might have expected the present to correspond with ἐπιθυμεῖ.

οὐδὲ—οὗ negatives both the μέν and the δέ clause, 'nor do I converse if I receive payment and decline to converse if I am not paid'.

[33 B] 15 παρέχω—ἐρωτᾶν - 'I submit to be questioned', lit. 'I offer myself for questioning'. Greek often has the infinitive active, as a verbal noun in the dative, where English uses the infinitive passive, but in some phrases, e.g. καλὸς ἰδεῖν, 'fair to see', the active is used in both languages.

16 καὶ—λέγω - sc. παρέχω ἐμαυτὸν ἐρωτᾶν; 'and also if anyone wishes to listen as the man who answers to what I have to say'.

17 τούτων τις are to be taken together, 'if any of these'.

18 τὴν αἰτίαν ὑπέχοιμι - 'I could not fairly have the blame laid at my door', sc. if any disciple turns out badly. Socrates is thinking of Alcibiades and Critias, two most distinguished followers who turned out very badly.

ὧν goes with μηδενί.

19 μήτε - not οὔτε, because Socrates is talking of the whole class of his disciples: see on 21 D ἃ μὴ οἶδα.

21 ἄλλοι πάντες - 'any other men'. Another reading is οἱ ἄλλοι πάντες, which would mean 'all the rest'.

CHAPTER XXII

[33 c] 3 ὅτι - 'because', answers the question 'why?' διὰ τί;

4 ἐξεταζομένοις - The cause of rejoicing after χαίρω is often put in the dative. 'They rejoice in the examination of those who think that they are wise.'

8 θεία μοῖρα - 'divine dispensation'. We might have expected παντὶ ἄλλῳ τρόπῳ, but 'every way by which any other divine dispensation ordained' is equivalent to 'any other way by which a divine', etc.

9 καί emphasises ὁτιοῦν, 'anything whatever'.

[33D] 11 χρῆν - ἄν is commonly omitted with verbs of necessity and possibility in unfulfilled conditional sentences.

12 εἴτε τινές - The main protasis εἰ—διαφθείρω is subdivided into two parts, one beginning with εἴτε τινές, the other with εἰ δὲ μή instead of a second εἴτε, since the second alternative, namely that those corrupted by Socrates will not appear in person, is the more likely: εἴπερ—ἐπεπόνθεσαν is a variaton on the original protasis εἰ—διαφθείρω.

14 αὐτούς is emphatic: tr. 'coming forward in person'.

15 τῶν οἰκείων—ἐκείνων - 'some of their relatives'. ἐκείνων depends on τῶν οἰκείων, lit. 'some of the relatives of them'.

20 Κρίτων - One of Socrates' most devoted friends. In the Crito he is represented as trying to persuade Socrates to escape from prison.

21 ἐμός—δημότης - Socrates belonged to the deme Ἀλωπεκή of the tribe Ἀντιοχίς.

Κριτόβουλος and his father were present at Socrates' death. Many of the persons mentioned in this chapter are not known.

[33E] 22 ὁ Σφήττιος - 'of the deme Sphettus'. Aeschines was a writer of dialogues. Epigenes was present at Socrates' death.

23 ὁ Κηφισιεύς - 'of the deme Cephisia'. τοίνυν marks a transition: 'yes and these others'.

26 ἐκεῖνός γε - 'he', the dead Theodotus.

27 καταδεηθείη - 'entreat him', sc. not to give evidence against Socrates. Demodocus entrusted his son Theages to the care of Socrates.

[34A] 29 Ἀδείμαντος - brother of Plato: he is one of the characters in the Republic.

30 **Ἀπολλόδωρος** - A very emotional friend of Socrates, nicknamed ὁ μανικός, 'the madman'.

32 **μάλιστα μέν** - 'by rights', indicating the best course: εἰ δὲ ἐπελάθετο gives the inferior alternative.

34 **παραχωρῶ** - 'I make way', sc. for you on the platform.

35 **τούτου πᾶν τοὐναντίον** is in apposition to the sentence: see on 25 B.

[34 B] 38 **αὐτοὶ—λόγον ἔχοιεν** - 'There would perhaps be some sense in it, if those who had actually been corrupted helped me'; lit. 'the corrupted themselves would perhaps have reason if they helped me'; see on 31 B.

40 **τίνα ἄλλον—ἀλλ' ἤ** - 'what other reason have they for helping me unless it is'. For ἀλλ' ἤ, 'unless', see 20 D.

42 **ξυνίσασι—ψευδομένῳ** - 'they are aware that Meletus is lying', lit. 'are aware of M. lying'. ξύνοιδα takes a dative completed by a participle.

CHAPTER XXIII

[34 C] 3 **ἀναμνησθεὶς ἑαυτοῦ** - 'remembering his own behaviour' (on some occasion when he was on trial), lit. 'remembering himself'.

4 **εἰ ὁ μέν** - εἰ and not ὅτι is regular after ἀγανακτεῖν. Greek says, 'I am indignant', or 'I wonder, if', not 'that'. ὁ μέν is τις of l. 3. The μέν clause is subordinate, as often: 'that, though he when being tried in a case actually' (καί) 'less serious than this one', etc. 'I positively' (ἄρα, expressing surprise) 'do none of these things'. ἐδεήθη is indicative, referring to a past fact; see on ἔμενον, 28 E.

6 **παιδία—ἀναβιβασάμενος** - It was correct for defendants to produce their children in court to excite the compassion of the jury. Aristophanes and in imitation of him the French poet Racine parody this by introducing the puppies of a dog who is on trial.

9 **καὶ ταῦτα** - 'and that too', 'notwithstanding'; a common phrase.

ὡς ἂν δόξαιμι - 'as I might be in his eyes' (lit. 'as I might seem to be') κινδυνεύων τὸν ἔσχατον κίνδυνον.

11 **αὐθαδέστερον—σχοίη** - 'might stiffen himself against me', lit. 'might be in a more stubborn state'.

12 **αὐτοῖς τούτοις** - neuter, 'just for this very reason'.

87

[34D] 13 **οὐκ ἀξιῶ—δ' οὖν -** 'mind, I am not saying that anyone is, but assuming that there is somebody' (in this position).

14 **ἄν** goes with λέγειν.

16 **τοῦτο—'Ομήρου -** 'in these very words of Homer': the phrase is in apposition to the sentence. The reference is to *Od.* XIX. 163 οὐ γὰρ ἀπὸ δρυός ἐσσι παλαιφάτου οὐδ' ἀπὸ πέτρης (ἐσσι, 'thou art', παλαίφατος, 'ancient').

18 **ὥστε—εἰσι -** 'so that I too have relatives'. τρεῖς is emphatic, 'three of them'.

[34E] 23 **ἀλλ' εἰ μὲν—πρὸς δ' οὖν -** To correspond with the participle αὐθαδιζόμενος, we should expect something like 'but being courageous and thinking it unseemly', etc. We have, however, the less boastful expression, 'but if I am courageous', etc., 'never mind' (ἄλλος λόγος, lit. 'that is another matter'), 'but at any rate, for my credit and yours', etc.

26 **τοῦτο τοὔνομα -** sc. the name of 'wise'.

27 **ἀλλ' οὖν δεδογμένον γε -** 'at all events people are bent on believing'.

[35A] 31 **τοιοῦτοι ἔσονται -** 'are to behave in this fashion'.

32 **δοκοῦντας μέν τι εἶναι -** 'persons of standing', lit. 'seeming to be somewhat'. **θαυμάσια δὲ ἐργαζομένους -** 'behaving surprisingly', is an idiom equivalent to our 'leaving no stone unturned'.

33 **ὡς—οἰομένους** go together, 'as thinking that they will suffer a calamity'.

34 **ὥσπερ—ἐσομένων -** sc. the same people as οἰομένους, but the case is changed to gen. absolute, as we now have Socrates' explanation of their conduct.

37 **οἱ διαφέροντες 'Αθηναίων -** 'those of the Athenians who excel'.

38 **εἰς -** 'in respect of', as in 29D.

[35B] 41 **τοὺς δοκοῦντας—εἶναι -** 'who have even the smallest reputation'.

42 **ὑμᾶς -** Supply χρή.

44 **εἰσάγοντος** is an appropriate word, as εἰσάγειν means both 'to bring into court', and also 'to bring on the stage'.

CHAPTER XXIV

1 **οὐδὲ δίκαιον—εἶναι** - 'I do not think it just either'; i.e. 'I think it unjust as well as dishonourable'.

[35 C] 3 **ἀποφεύγειν** - 'to be acquitted' serves as the passive of ἀποψηφίζεσθαι; see on 17 A πάσχειν and ποιεῖν.

4 **ἐπὶ τούτῳ** refers forward to ἐπὶ—τὰ δίκαια.

καταχαρίζεσθαι - 'to give away *wrongfully*' (κατά).

5 **ταῦτα** - sc. τὰ δίκαια, 'to decide the right'. δίκαια is legal as well as moral right.

6 **ὀμώμοκεν οὐ** - οὐ is used instead of μή, perhaps in order to bring forward vividly the words of the oath.

9 **ἀξιοῦτε** - ἀξιοῦν hardly means more than 'think' and therefore can be followed by δεῖν, 'think that I must'. Its original meaning, 'think it worthy' or 'right', would make δεῖν superfluous.

[35 D] 11 **μήτε ὅσια** - being forbidden by the juryman's oath.

μέντοι is a strong affirmative particle, 'yes, by Zeus'.

14 **τῷ δεῖσθαι βιαζοίμην** - 'constrain you by entreaties'.

15 **ὑμᾶς** is the object of διδάσκειν.

ἀτεχνῶς—ἐμαυτοῦ - 'my defence would be literally an accusation against myself'.

PART II

After the Verdict

(Second Speech)

The jury in the trial of Socrates numbered 501. He was found guilty by 281 votes to 220. At Athens in a prosecution for impiety the penalty was not fixed by law beforehand, but determined by the jury in accordance with the assessment of the prosecutor or defendant. Such a suit was called an ἀγὼν τίμητος (a suit to be assessed); in an ἀγὼν ἀτίμητος the penalty was fixed by law beforehand. After the verdict 'guilty', Meletus made a second speech, demanding the penalty (τίμησις) of death. Socrates replies, ch. xxv–xxviii, with the counter-proposal (ἀντιτίμησις) of a fine. The jury were obliged to choose between these two proposals.

CHAPTER XXV

[35 E]   1 τὸ μὲν μὴ ἀγανακτεῖν is a sort of object to ξυμβάλλεται. Strictly we ought to have εἰς τὸ μέν κτλ. Socrates
begins: 'My lack of indignation...many other circumstances
contribute to it', as if he had at first thought of saying: 'my
lack of indignation...is caused by many other circumstances', and had changed the construction in the middle of
the sentence.

[36 A]   3 καί—γέγονεν - Another slight change of construction. Strictly we ought to have καὶ τοῦτο ὅτι—γέγονεν,
'many other circumstances...and also this one, namely,
that', etc.

5 ἑκατέρων—ἀριθμόν - 'the actual number of votes on each
side'.

6 οὕτω—ἔσεσθαι - 'that it would be so close', lit. 'so within
a little'. παρά sometimes expresses the difference short of or
beyond a given mark.

7 τριάκοντα - A round number. 31 votes would have had to
be transferred to Socrates, to produce a majority of one in his
favour.

8 μετέπεσον - 'had changed sides' serves as the passive to
μετέθεσαν: see on 17 A.

Μέλητον—ἀποπέφευγα. Socrates contends that Meletus,
being one of three prosecutors, has only gained one-third of
the 281 votes given for a verdict of 'guilty'.

11 ἀνέβη - ἀνέβησαν would have been more strictly grammatical
to correspond with the plural κατηγορήσοντες.

κἂν ὦφλε—τῶν ψήφων - In a criminal trial the prosecutor, if he failed to obtain one-fifth of the votes cast, was fined
1,000 drachmae (about £40) and forbidden to bring any such
actions for the future. 501 votes were cast. Socrates assigns
93⅔ to Meletus as his share—less than one-fifth of the whole.

[36 B]   12 τὸ πέμπτον μέρος - τό signifies 'the *well-known* 5th
part'.

CHAPTER XXVI

1 τιμᾶται—θανάτου - 'proposes death as the penalty'. The
penalty is put as a genitive of price, here and below ll. 2 and 3.

2 τίνος ὑμῖν ἀντιτιμήσομαι - 'what will you have me

propose as the counter-penalty?' lit. 'at what shall I fix the counter-penalty for you?'

3 **τῆς ἀξίας** - Supply τιμῆς, 'the right penalty', 'what I deserve.'

4 **παθεῖν ἢ ἀποτῖσαι** - παθεῖν of death, imprisonment, exile, etc.: ἀποτῖσαι of fines. A technical legal phrase.

ὅ τι μαθών - 'because', an idiomatic phrase. τί μαθὼν φιλεῖς; = 'what induces you to love?' lit. 'having learnt what do you love?' ὅ τι is the indirect form of the interrogative, and like Lat. *quod* comes to mean 'in that'. οὐ σοφὸς εἶ ὅ τι μαθὼν φιλεῖς, 'you are not wise, in that you are induced' (or 'for being induced') 'to love', i.e. 'because you love'.

5 **ὧνπερ οἱ πολλοί** - sc. ἐπιμελοῦνται.

7 **ξυνωμοσιῶν** - 'political clubs'. Clubs of a revolutionary character were prevalent at Athens at the end of the 5th cent.

τῶν ἐν τῇ πόλει γιγνομένων - 'everything that goes on in the city'. τῶν ἄλλων is neuter, and τῶν—γιγνομένων refers back to it.

8 **ἡγησάμενος ἐμαυτὸν—ἐπιεικέστερον** - ἡγησάμενος ἐπιεικέστερος εἶναι would be more usual and not quite so emphatic.

9 **ἐπιεικέστερον ἢ ὥστε** - 'too upright to', 'too honest to'.

[36C] 9 **σῴζεσθαι** - In 31D Socrates said that he would have perished long since, if he had taken part in politics. He there meant that his independent honesty would have brought him to grief; here he is thinking of the questionable conduct of conventional politicians, who obtain advancement at the expense of their conscience.

11 **ἐπὶ—ἐπιχειρῶν** - 'but entering on the task' (ἰὼν ἐπὶ) 'of doing the greatest services' (τὸ εὐεργετεῖν τὴν μεγίστην εὐεργεσίαν) 'in private life to each individual' (ἰδίᾳ ἕκαστον), 'as I say, I entered on the task (ἐνταῦθα ᾖα) of trying', etc. After ἰὼν ἐπὶ τὸ—εὐεργετεῖν we should expect, 'this is what I did—I tried', etc. But ἐνταῦθα ᾖα is written to correspond with ἐνταῦθα μὲν οὐκ ᾖα, l. 10. ἐνταῦθα ᾖα refers forward to ἐπιχειρῶν. It would be easier if ἰών were absent, and many editors cut it out.

14 **τῶν—μηδενός** - 'none of his own affairs'.

πρὶν—ἐπιμεληθείη - In direct speech this would be πρὶν ἂν σαυτοῦ ἐπιμελήθῃς.

15 ὅπως—ἔσοιτο = ὅπως ἔσει of direct speech.

[36D] 19 εἰ δεῖ γε—τιμᾶσθαι - 'if I must propose' (εἰ—γε marks that he is compelled to by the law) 'a penalty in accordance with my true deserts'.

20 καὶ ταῦτά γε - 'yes, moreover, and'.

22 ἐπί - 'with a view to'.

23 μᾶλλον—πρέπει [οὕτως] ὡς - If οὕτως be cut out, ὡς must mean 'than', as it does occasionally in good authors. If οὕτως is kept, we have something like the Scottish idiom 'fully nearer', a mixture of 'fully as near as', and 'nearer'; here the mixture is 'there is nothing which is fully as fitting as' (πρέπει οὕτως ὡς) and 'which is more fitting (μᾶλλον πρέπει).

25 πρυτανείῳ - The Prytaneum (not the same as the θόλος 32 C) was a building on the north-east slope of the Acropolis, sacred to the goddess Hestia, which contained the common hearth of the city. Ambassadors and distinguished citizens were entertained there, among them victors at the Olympian and other great games.

26 ἵππῳ—ζεύγει - ἵππος is a single horse, ξυνωρίς, a pair; ζεῦγος, four abreast.
'Ολυμπίασιν - 'at Olympia', an old locative case.

28 ὁ μὲν—δεῖται - Only rich men could afford to enter for chariot-races, and they would not need public support. Socrates, however, was poor; see 23 C.

CHAPTER XXVII

[37A] 2 οἴκτου - the 'lamentations' scorned in ch. XXIII.

3 τὸ δὲ οὐκ ἔστιν—τοιοῦτον - 'but really it is not so': τὸ δέ is demonstrative as in 23A (where see note), but seems here to be the subject of ἔστι.

5 ἑκὼν εἶναι - 'willingly', goes with ἀδικεῖν, and limits it. This phrase and similar ones, e.g. ὀλίγου δεῖν, have come to be simply adverbs. πέπεισμαι = 'I have made up my mind', and is naturally followed by μηδένα, not οὐδένα, as μή is the normal negative with the infinitive when not in indirect speech.

7 ὥσπερ—ἀνθρώποις - e.g. at Sparta. This remark would not tend to win the favour of Socrates' judges.

8 μίαν ἡμέραν - 'for one day'; accusative of duration of time.

[37B] 13 **τοῦ κακοῦ** - Notice that τον has no accent and stands therefore for τινός, 'any'.

14 **τί δείσας** - sc. τιμήσομαι;

15 **φημί** - in 29A ff.

16 **ἔχωμαι—ὄντων** - 'shall I lay hold on what I well know are evils?' ὧν is put by attraction for τούτων ἅ, and κακῶν ὄντων is curiously attracted to ὧν. (1) ἃ εὖ οἶδ' ὅτι κακά ἐστι might be replaced by (2) ἃ εὖ οἶδα κακὰ ὄντα, and by attraction this would become ὧν εὖ οἶδα κακῶν ὄντων. (1) and (2) have been fused together, and the result is ὧν εὖ οἶδ' ὅτι κακῶν ὄντων. οἶδ' ὅτι not infrequently = οἶδα. ἕλωμαί τι "shall I choose one of what I well know to be evils?' is another reading.

17 **τοῦ τιμησάμενος** - 'proposing what penalty?' lit. 'fixing the penalty at what?' τοῦ is interrogative and = τίνος.

[37C] 18 **τῇ ἀεί—τοῖς ἕνδεκα** - 'to the persons bearing office in succession' (ἀεί, 'from time to time', 'constantly') 'the Eleven'. The Eleven were a board of ten elected annually by lot, together with a clerk (γραμματεύς). Their business was to take charge of prisons and see that sentences of death were carried out.

19 **χρημάτων—ἐκτίσω** - 'a fine and imprisonment until I pay it'. δεδέσθαι, 'to be kept in prison'.

21 **νῦν δή** - 'just now', to be distinguished from νῦν δέ, 'as it is'. **ὁπόθεν ἐκτίσω** - 'to pay with', lit. 'whence I shall pay'. ἐκτίσω is future indicative.

22 **ἄν—τιμήσαιτε** - 'you might fix'. The active is used of the jury, the middle of the prosecutor and defendant.

24 **εἰ—εἰμι** - 'if, as you say, I am': see note on 25B, εἰ—διαφθείρω, a similar form of conditional sentence.

25 **ὅτι ὑμεῖς μὲν—οἴσουσι ῥᾳδίως** - We should expect after 'that you cannot endure my conversation and discussions' something like 'and that other people can still less put up with them'. We find instead a sudden and very effective question, 'will other people then be content to put up with them?'

[37D] 27 **βαρύτεραι—καὶ ἐπιφθονώτεραι** - 'too tedious and objectionable', sc. to be borne. The adjectives agree with διατριβάς; the masculine λόγους is added as an explanation.

28 **ἄρα** expresses surprise as in 34C.

30 **ἐξελθόντι** - ἐξέρχομαι (inf. ἐξιέναι), 'I go into exile'; φεύγω, 'I live in exile'; κατέρχομαι (inf. κατιέναι), 'I return from exile'.

31 ἄλλην—ἀμειβομένῳ - 'going from one city to another', lit. 'changing to one city from another'.

33 τούτους - sc. οἱ νέοι.

CHAPTER XXVIII

[37E] 2 οὐχ οἷός τ'—ζῆν - 'Can we not get you to go away and live?' ἡμῖν is the ethic dative, indicating the speaker's interest in the subject.

4 τινας ὑμῶν - 'some of you', meaning nearly all. Compare καὶ ἄλλος τις 30D.

6 ὡς εἰρωνευομένῳ - 'as believing me to be insincere'. 'Irony' means regularly 'self-depreciation' or 'mock modesty'. The most conspicuous instance of the irony of Socrates is his constant profession of ignorance.

[38A] 7 ὅτι καὶ τυγχάνει-'that it also happens to be'; Socrates adopted his mode of life not only because his duty bade him not neglect the god's command, but also (καί) because such a life was in accordance with his highest interests as a human being.

11 ταῦτα δ' - δέ recapitulates the clause ὁ δὲ ἀνεξέταστος—ἀνθρώπῳ; see 32D τούτου δέ.

12 τὰ δὲ—οὕτως - 'but indeed it is so'. τά is demonstrative and the subject to ἔχει, like τὸ δέ 37A.

14 εἰ μὲν γὰρ ἦν - γάρ = 'no doubt'. The connexion of thought is: 'I should be quite willing to propose a penalty, if I could find one which would do me no harm, *for* if I had money', etc.

[38B] 16 ὅσα ἔμελλον ἐκτίσειν - 'as much as I should have been in a position to pay'. ἔμελλον is part of the conditional sentence as in 20A.

17 οὐ γὰρ ἔστιν - 'no, I have none'. To complete the thought we can supply οὐ τιμῶμαι, 'I do not propose a penalty, for I have none', but in Greek the consciousness of an ellipse in such cases hardly exists. So ἀλλὰ γάρ, 'but really', 19C, and often.

εἰ μὴ ἄρα - 'unless indeed'; see 17B.

19 μνᾶν ἀργυρίου - about £4. Xenophon tells us that Socrates possessed about £20 in all.

22 αὐτοὶ δ' ἐγγυᾶσθαι - 'they say that they stand surety'.

PART III

After the Sentence

(Third Speech)

The jury pronounced sentence of death. Diogenes Laertius II. 42 tells us that the majority was increased by 80 votes.

CHAPTER XXIX

[38C]   1 **οὐ—χρόνου -** 'it is for the sake of only a short gain in time'. As Socrates was 70, his death might be expected to come soon in the course of nature.

 2 **ὄνομα—ἀπεκτόνατε -** 'you will have the name and the blame of having put Socrates to death, from those who wish to abuse the city'. ὄνομα ἕξετε καὶ αἰτίαν is equivalent to a passive verb, 'you will be reputed blameworthy, because you have', etc. Hence ὑπό is used.

 7 **τοῦτο -** sc. my death.

 8 **τοῦ βίου -** with πόρρω, 'far advanced in years'.

[38D]   12 **ἑαλωκέναι -** 'to have been convicted'. ἁλίσκομαι, perf. ἑάλωκα, serves as the passive of αἱρέω, 'I convict'. **τοιούτων** goes with λόγων.

 13 **ἅπαντα—λέγειν -** 'to do and say anything' (no matter how degrading).

 15 **τόλμης -** 'audacity', in a bad sense.

 17 **θρηνοῦντός τέ μου—λέγοντος** explains οἷ' ἄν—ἀκούειν. ἀκούειν takes an accusative of things, but a genitive of persons. Hence οἷ' ἄν, and θρηνοῦντός τέ μου, not θρηνοῦντά τέ με.

[38E]   19 **οἷα—ἀκούειν -** See last note.

 23 **ἐκείνως -** sc. by making an undignified defence with tears and entreaties.

[39A]   25 **ἀποφεύξεται—θάνατον -** πᾶν ποιῶν, 'at any cost'. θάνατον is object to ἀποφεύξεται.

 27 **τό γε ἀποθανεῖν—ἐκφύγοι -** 'a man may at least escape from death'. γε implies 'but not from dishonour'. **καὶ—καὶ -** 'both—and'.

 30 **τολμᾷ -** 'has the audacity'; see above, τόλμης, l. 15.

 31 **μὴ οὐ—χαλεπόν -** 'I suspect that this is not what is difficult'. In Plato μή with the subjunctive expresses a cautious assertion.

32 **πονηρίαν** - Supply ἐκφυγεῖν.

33 **θᾶττον γὰρ θανάτου θεῖ** - Note the alliteration; 'for it flies faster than fate' (Dyer).

[39B] 34 **ὑπὸ τοῦ βραδυτέρου** - 'by the slower', sc. death.

35 **δεινοὶ καὶ ὀξεῖς** - 'clever and sharp'.

36 **ὑφ᾽ ὑμῶν—ὀφλών** - ὑπό is used because δίκην ὀφλεῖν is a passive verb, 'to be condemned to', like ὄνομα ἕξετε above, l. 2. The full meaning of θανάτου—ὀφλών is 'having lost a suit, where death is the penalty'.

38 **ὠφληκότες μοχθηρίαν** - ὀφλισκάνειν alone, without δίκην, comes to mean 'to be condemned', and the charge of which the accused is found guilty is put in the accusative; 'you will be guilty of wickedness and injustice in the eyes of truth'. ὠφληκότες, perf. participle, indicates a continuing state, ὀφλών, a single occasion (like τεθνάναι, 'to be dead', ἀποθανεῖν 'to die').

39 **καὶ οὗτοι** - Supply ἐμμένουσι; 'and they abide by their sentence', namely disgrace.

ταῦτα—σχεῖν - 'maybe' (που ἴσως) 'this was inevitably bound to happen so'.

40 **μετρίως ἔχειν** - 'it is well'.

CHAPTER XXX

1 **τὸ—μετὰ τοῦτο** - 'in the next place'; an adverbial phrase.

[39C] 4 **ὅταν—ἀποθανεῖσθαι** - It is a widespread belief among primitive races that men who are near death have the gift of prophecy.

4 **φημὶ γάρ** - 'now I say', as γάρ in 20E, etc.

6 **ἢ οἵαν—ἀπεκτόνατε** - A short way of saying 'than the punishment which you inflicted upon me by putting me to death'; in full the Greek would be ἢ οἵαν τιμωρίαν ἐμὲ ἀποκτείνοντες ἐτιμωρήσασθε. So in colloquial English we say: 'he wore a coat much longer than his father'.

8 **τὸ δὲ—ἀποβήσεται** - 'but you will find the result very different'. τό is demonstrative, as in 37A.

9 **πλείους ἔσονται** - This clause explains τὸ δὲ—ἀποβήσεται, and so has no conjunction. See 22A οἱ μὲν μάλιστα.

11 **οὐκ ἠσθάνεσθε** - sc. that I kept them in check.

[39D] 14 **τινά** - 'people', like ἄλλος τις (30D). τινά is the object to ἐπισχήσειν.

96

15 αὕτη ἡ ἀπαλλαγή - 'that way of escape', sc. from giving an account of your life, by putting people to death.

οὔτε πάνυ - 'not remarkably', lit. 'not altogether', like οὐ πάνυ (19A).

17 μὴ—κολούειν - 'not to suppress others'.

CHAPTER XXXI

[39E]   2 ὑπὲρ—πράγματος - 'on behalf of this thing which has come to pass'. ὑπέρ is more than 'about'. Socrates wishes to reconcile the minority in his favour to the verdict, by showing that for him death is no evil.

3 οἱ ἄρχοντες - 'the Eleven'.

ἀσχολίαν ἄγουσι - 'are busy', no doubt with arrangements for taking Socrates to prison.

οἱ - sc. to the prison.

5 τοσοῦτον χρόνον - 'till then', i.e. till the Eleven are ready.

διαμυθολογῆσαι - 'tell our fancies', sc. about the other world. διά implies interchange of talk.

[40A]   8 τί ποτε νοεῖ - 'what it means'.

10 ἡ τοῦ δαιμονίου - see 31 D and Introduction.

12 πάνυ ἐπὶ σμικροῖς - 'on quite small matters'.

14 ἅ γε δὴ—νομίζεται - The subject to νομίζεται is ταῦτα or a similar pronoun, to be supplied from ἅ γε. Where English idiom repeats a relative after a conjunction, Greek uses a demonstrative pronoun in the second clause. English says: 'whom we thought wise and whom we loved', Greek, 'whom we thought wise, and we loved him'.

[40B]   17 ἀνέβαινον ἐνταυθοῖ - 'was coming before the court here': see on ἀναβέβηκα (17D).

19 λέγοντα μεταξύ - 'in the act of speaking'. Grammatically μεταξύ qualifies ἐπέσχε, lit. 'checked me in the middle as I was speaking'.

22 κινδυνεύει γάρ - γάρ is introductory, and not to be translated. So too γάρ in l. 26 and ch. xxxii, l. 3.

[40C]   26 οὐ γάρ—οὐκ - 'assuredly', lit. 'it is not possible that—not'.

27 τι—ἀγαθὸν πράξειν - 'to fare well in some way' = εὖ τι πράξειν.

CHAPTER XXXII

3 **οἷον μηδὲν—τεθνεῶτα** - 'like being nothing, and the dead man's having no sensation of anything'. The construction in full is τοιοῦτόν ἐστιν οἷόν ἐστι μηδὲν εἶναι. τὸν τεθνεῶτα is the subject to ἔχειν; εἶναι has no definite subject.

5 **κατὰ τὰ λεγόμενα** - 'as the legends say', sc. in the poets and in the mysteries.

6 **τοῦ τόπου** goes with μεταβολή and μετοίκησις together, 'change and migration from the region here to another'.
ἐνθένδε - 'hence', is put instead of ἐνθάδε, 'here', as a terse and vivid way of saying, 'from here hence to another region'.

7 **καὶ εἴτε** - 'and if, on the one hand', is not answered until εἰ δ' αὖ, l. 20. εἴτε—ἐστιν, 'if it is' (implying 'as it is said to be'): see on εἰ—εἰμι (37c).

[40D] 9 **ἂν οἶμαι—οἶμαι ἂν** (l. 15)—**ἂν εὑρεῖν** (l. 16) - For ἄν repeated in a long conditional clause see on 17D. ἄν here belongs to εὑρεῖν in each case.
εἰ—ἐκλεξάμενον δέοι—καὶ—δέοι - δέοι is repeated to help the memory in the long sentence.

13 **σκεψάμενον εἰπεῖν** - 'to reflect and say'. ἐκλεξάμενον and ἀντιπαραθέντα are subordinate to these words: lit. 'if a man were compelled to pick out, etc....to compare, etc....and after consideration' (σκεψάμενον) 'to say'.

15 **μὴ ὅτι** 'not only'. In full the construction is μὴ ὑπολάβητε ὅτι λέγω - 'don't suppose that I mean'.

16 **τὸν μέγαν βασιλέα** - 'the Great King', i.e. the King of Persia, who was the proverbial example of the most fortunate human being.

[40E] 17 **αὐτόν** - 'himself', sc. the Great King. Others take αὐτόν as summing up μὴ ὅτι—βασιλέα, 'not only a private individual, but the Great King—he would find them easy to count'. The first interpretation seems the simpler and better.

19 **οὕτω δή** - 'in this way', sc. if we are unconscious after death.

22 **ἄρα** - 'after all', expressing some surprise.

24 **εἰς "Αιδου** - Supply 'the house of'.

[41A] 26 **Μίνως τε— Τριπτόλεμος** - Minos, Rhadamanthys and Aeacus, sons of Zeus, are the usual legendary judges in the underworld. Triptolemus, son of the King of Eleusis, does not seem to be mentioned elsewhere as a judge below, though he is spoken of in the Homeric hymn to Demeter as a judge on earth, and appears in some vase-paintings of Hades along with Aeacus and Rhadamanthys. It is customary in speaking of famous legendary or historical personages to use the article with their names in Greek. By omitting the article Socrates playfully implies that he will be on intimate terms with these heroes.

29 **Ὀρφεῖ—Μουσαίῳ** are the two great mythical bards.

30 **Ἡσιόδῳ καὶ Ὁμήρῳ** - 'Hesiod and Homer', the epic poets.

31 **ἐπὶ πόσῳ—ὑμῶν** - 'what would not some of you give for that?' lit. 'at what price would any of you accept that?' English idiom uses an exclamation, Greek puts the thought in the form of a question. For τις implying several people see on 30D and 39D.

32 **ἔμοιγε καὶ αὐτῷ** - 'for myself especially'.

[41 B] 34 **Παλαμήδει** - See Virg. *Aen.* II. 81 ff. Palamedes was falsely accused of treason by Odysseus; he was condemned and executed. Several plays were written on his story.

Αἴαντι - Ajax killed himself from mortification, when the arms of Achilles were, as he thought, unjustly awarded to Odysseus and not to him. The story is well known from the *Ajax* of Sophocles. Socrates is especially interested in Palamedes and Ajax as fellow-victims with him of injustice.

36 **ἀντιπαραβάλλοντι** - It is somewhat awkward to have no conjunction joining this clause to what precedes, but the omission may be accounted for as Socrates is explaining more precisely than in θαυμαστὴ—αὐτόθι what he will do when he meets Palamedes and Ajax: see on 22A and 39C. There are various ways of punctuating the passage, but none is free from difficulty.

37 **καὶ δὴ καί** introduces the climax. See on 26D.

τὸ μέγιστον is in apposition to the sentence.

39 **διάγειν** depends on οὐκ ἂν ἀηδὲς εἴη l. 37; its subject is ἐμέ understood, agreeing with ἐξετάζοντα and ἐρευνῶντα on which the interrogative clauses τίς αὐτῶν—ἔστιν δ' οὐ depend; 'and, moreover, above all [it would be no small pleasure] to pass my time examining and enquiring of those of the other world' (τοὺς ἐκεῖ) 'as of those here, which of them is wise'.

42 **Σίσυφον** - a legendary king of Corinth, notorious for treachery and deceit.

[41 C] 42 **ἢ ἄλλους—ἄν τις εἴποι** - 'or one might mention

7-2

numbers more'; μύριοι is used for any indefinitely large number.

44 **ἀμήχανον—εὐδαιμονίας** - 'an infinite delight', lit. 'an impracticable amount of happiness'.

45 **πάντως—ἀποκτείνουσι** - 'At all events assuredly they do not yonder put men to death for doing that' (sc. for conversing and cross-questioning).

CHAPTER XXXIII

2 **ἕν τι—ἀληθές** - 'to consider this one thing which is true', lit. 'to consider one thing, this, a true point'. The position of both τοῦτο and ἀληθές is emphatic, like that of δίκαιον in 18 A.

[41 D] 5 **τὰ ἐμά** - 'what has happened to me'.

7 **τεθνάναι καὶ ἀπηλλάχθαι** - 'to be dead and free from trouble'. The perfect infinitives indicate a continuing state. πράγματα in the plural often means 'troublesome business'.
βέλτιον ἦν - 'it was better', sc. in the minds of the gods, when they made their decision about my fate.

10 **οὐ πάνυ** - 'far from'; see on 19 A.

12 **τοῦτο—μέμφεσθαι** - 'for this they deserve to be blamed', lit. 'this is a worthy thing to blame them for'.

14 **τιμωρήσασθε** - 'take your revenge upon them', ironical.

20 **δίκαια πεπονθώς** - 'I shall have received my deserts'.

[42 A] 23 **ἀλλὰ γάρ** - 'but really', as in 19 C.

23 **πλὴν ἤ** - πλὴν ἤ is a little less emphatic than πλὴν by itself; 'except indeed to God'.

VOCABULARY

ABBREVIATIONS

acc.	accusative	interrog.	interrogative
act.	active	mid.	middle
adj.	adjective	neg.	negative
adv.	adverb	neut.	neuter
aor.	aorist	nom.	nominative
aux.	auxiliary	opt.	optative
comp.	comparative	partic.	participle
conj.	conjunction	pass.	passive
contr.	contracted	pers.	person
dat.	dative	pf.	perfect
d.	deponent	plup.	pluperfect
fem.	feminine	plur.	plural
fut.	future	prep.	preposition
gen.	genitive	pres.	present
i.	intransitive	pron.	pronoun
imper.	imperative	rel.	relative
impers.	impersonal	str.	strong
impf.	imperfect	subj.	subjunctive
ind.	indicative	superl.	superlative
indecl.	indeclinable	t.	transitive
inf.	infinitive	v.	verb
interj.	interjection	voc.	vocative

The principal parts of compound verbs are, except when otherwise stated, given under the heading of the simple verbs, if they have any irregularity. The term 'transitive' is here used only for verbs which take an object in the accusative.

ἀβρύνω, v.t. *deck out*; mid. *give oneself airs*

ἀγαθ-ός, -ή, -όν (borrowed comp. ἀμείνων or βελτίων, superl. ἄριστος or βέλτιστος), *good, noble, brave*

ἀγανακτέω, v.i. *be vexed* (with dat.)

ἀ-γνοέω, v.t. *know not, be ignorant*

ἀγορ-ά ἡ, -ας, *market-place*

ἄγροικ-ος, -ον, adj. *rustic, blunt*

ἄγω, v.t., fut. ἄξω, aor.
ἤγαγον, lead, bring

ἀγών ὁ, -ος, contest, trial

ἀγωνίζομαι, v.d.t. and i.
fight, contend in

'Ἀδείμαντ-ος ὁ, -ον,
Adimantus

ἀδελφ-ός ὁ, -οῦ, brother

ἄ-δηλ-ος, -ον, adj. not clear;
hidden from (with dat.)

ἀ-διά-φθαρτ-ος, -ον, adj.
uncorrupted

ἀ-δικέω, v.t. and i. wrong; be
unjust; do wrong

ἀ-δίκημα τό, -τος, wrong-
doing, crime

ἀδικί-α ἡ, -ας, injustice

ἄ-δικ-ος, -ον, adj. unjust; adv.
ἀδίκως

ἀεί, adv. always; at any time;
from time to time

ἀεροβατέω, v.i. walk the air

ἀ-ηδ-ής, -ές, adj. disagreeable

ἀ-θάνατ-ος, -ον, adj. immortal

ἄ-θε-ος, -ον, adj. denying the
gods; atheistical

'Ἀθηναῖ-ος, -α, -ον, adj.
Athenian

ἀθρό-ος, -α, -ον, adj. in
crowds; collectively

Αἰακ-ός ὁ, -οῦ, Aeacus

Αἰαντόδωρ-ος ὁ, -ον,
Aeantodorus

Αἴ-ας ὁ, -αντος, Ajax

"Ἀιδ-ης ὁ, -ον, Hades. ἐν
"Ἀιδου, in [the house of]
Hades

αἴνιγμα τό, -τος, enigma,
riddle

αἰνίττομαι, v.d.t. and i. talk
in riddles

αἱρέω, v.t., fut. αἱρήσω, aor.
εἷλον, pf. ᾕρηκα, take, seize;
convict; mid. choose

αἰσθάνομαι, v.d.t., fut.
αἰσθήσομαι, aor. ᾐσθόμην
pf. ᾔσθημαι, perceive

αἴσθησ-ις ἡ, -εως, perception

Αἰσχίν-ης ὁ, -ου, Aeschines

αἰσχρ-ός, -ά, -όν, adj. shameful, disgraceful

αἰσχύνομαι, v. pass., aor.
ᾐσχύνθην, be ashamed, feel
shame

αἰτέω, v.t. ask, request

αἰτί-α ἡ, -ας, blame; accusation; crime; cause

αἴτι-ον τό, -ον, cause

ἀ-κολασί-α ἡ, -ας, wantonness

ἀ-κόλαστ-ος, -ον, adj. unre-
strained, wanton

ἀκούσι-ος, -ον, adj. un-
willing, involuntary

ἀκούω, v.t. and i., fut. ἀκού-
σομαι, aor. ἤκουσα, pf. ἀκή-
κοα, hear (with gen. of
person, acc. of thing)

ἀκροάομαι, v.d.i. listen to
(with dat.)

ἀκροατ-ής ὁ, -οῦ, hearer;
member of the audience

ἄκ-ων, -ουσα, ον, adj. unwilling

ἀλήθει-α ἡ, -ας, truth

ἀληθεύω, v.i. speak the truth

ἀληθ-ής, -ές, adj. true; adv.
ἀληθῶς, truly

ἀλίσκομαι, v. pass., fut. ἁλώ-
σομαι, aor., ἑάλων, pf.
ἑάλωκα, be taken; be found
guilty

ἀλλά, conj. but

102

ἀλλήλ-ους, -ας, -α, plur. adj.
(no nom.) *one another*
ἄλλοθι, adv. *elsewhere*
ἀλλοῖ-ος, -α, -ον, adj.
different
ἄλλ-ος, -η, -ο, *another, other*;
οἱ ἄλλοι, *the rest*; ἄλλο τι
ἤ, interrog. particle, expecting the answer *yes*, Lat.
nonne
ἄλλως, adv. *otherwise*
ἀ-λόγιστ-ος, -ον, adj. *un-
reasoning*
ἄ-λογ-ος, -ον, adj. *unreason-
able*; *unexpected*
ἅμα, adv. *at the same time,
together*
ἀ-μαθ-ής, -ές, adj. *ignorant*
ἀμαθί-α, ἡ, -ας, *ignorance*
ἁμάρτημα τό, -τος, *error,
fault*
ἀμείβω, v.t. *change*; mid. *re-
quite*; *change residence*
ἀμείνων. See ἀγαθός
ἀ-μέλει-α ἡ, -ας, *neglect*
ἀ-μελέω, v.i. *neglect* (with
gen.)
ἀ-μήχαν-ος, -ον, adj. *impracticable*; *inconceivable*
ἀμφί, prep. (usually with acc.
in prose) *around, about,
associated with*
Ἀμφίπολ-ις ἡ, -εως, *Amphipolis*
ἀμφισβητέω, v.i. *argue,
dispute*
ἀμφότερ-ος, -α, -ον, adj.
each of two; plur. *both*
ἄν, particle
(1) conditional, with
indic. opt. inf. or partic. in

the apodosis of a condi-
tional sentence
(2) indefinite, with relative or relative particle
with subj. ὃς ἄν, *whoever*
ἀνα-βαίνω, v.i., fut. -βήσομαι,
aor. ἀνέβην pf. -βέβηκα, *go up*
ἀνα-βιβάζω, v.t. *make to go
up*; mid. *bring up* (as
witness)
ἀνα-γιγνώσκω, v.t. *read*
ἀναγκάζω, v.t. *compel*
ἀναγκαῖ-ος, -α, -ον, adj.
necessary
ἀνάγκ-η ἡ, -ης, *necessity*
ἀνα-ζητέω, v.t. *seek out, enquire into*
ἀν-αιρέω, v.t. *take up*;
destroy; in aor. ἀνεῖλον (of
an oracle), *gave an answer*
ἀν-αισχυντί-α ἡ, -ας, *shame-
lessness*
ἀναίσχυντ-ος, -ον, adj.
shameless; adv. ἀναισχύντως
ἀνα-λαμβάνω, v.t. *take up
again, resume*
ἀνα-μιμνήσκω, v.t. *remind*;
mid. (aor. ἀνεμνήσθην) *re-
collect* (with gen.)
Ἀναξάγορ-ας ὁ, -ου,
Anaxagoras
ἀν-άξι-ος, -α, -ον, adj. *un-
worthy*
ἀνα-πείθω, v.t. *over-persuade*
ἀνα-πίμπλημι, v.t., fut.
-πλήσω, aor. ἀνέπλησα, pf.
ἀναπέπληκα, *fill up with*;
implicate in
ἀνα-φέρω, v.t., fut. ἀνοίσω,
refer

ἀνδρεί-α ἡ, -ας, courage

ἀν-έλεγκτ-ος, -ον, adj. not refuted; irrefutable

ἀν-ελεύθερ-ος, -ον, adj. illiberal, unbecoming

ἀν-έλπιστ-ος, -ον, adj. unexpected

ἀν-εξ-έταστ-ος, -ον, adj. unexamined

ἀν-ερωτάω, v.i. ask a question of

ἀν-έχω, v.i. endure (with gen.)

ἀνήρ ὁ, ἀνδρός, man

ἀν-ηρόμην, dep. aor. of ἀνερωτάω, enquire of

ἀνθρώπει-ος, -α, -ον, adj. human

ἀνθρώπιν-ος, -η, -ον, adj. human

ἄνθρωπ-ος ὁ, -ου, human being, man

ἀν-όσι-ος, -α, -ον, adj. unrighteous

ἀντ-εῖπον, used as aor. of ἀντι-λέγω, v.i. speak in answer, reply, gainsay

ἀντί, prep. with gen., in return for, instead of

ἀντι-βόλησ-ις ἡ, -εως, beseeching, entreaty

ἀντι-γραφ-ή ἡ, -ῆς, counterplea; affidavit

Ἀντιοχ-ίς ἡ, -ίδος, Antiochis

ἀντι-παρα-βάλλω, v.t. (for parts see διαβάλλω), put side by side; compare

ἀντι-παρα-τίθημι, v.t. set over against; compare

ἀντι-τιμάομαι, v.d.i. propose a counter-penalty

Ἀντιφ-ῶν ὁ, -ῶντος, Antiphon

ἀντωμοσί-α ἡ, -ας, affidavit

Ἄνυτ-ος ὁ, -ου, Anytus

ἄξι-ος, -α, -ον, adj. worthy; with gen. worth; adv. ἀξίως

ἀξιό-χρε-ως, -ων, adj. (Attic declension), worthy of credit

ἀξιόω, v.t. think worthy; think right, deign; believe, request

ἀπ-άγω, v.t. lead away; arrest summarily

ἀπ-αλλαγ-ή ἡ, -ῆς, deliverance; way of escape

ἀπ-αλλάττω, v.t., fut. -αλλάξω, set free; pass. (str. aor. ἀπηλλάγην) be rid of; mid. take one's departure

ἀπ-αναισχυντέω, v.t. deny shamelessly

ἅπας, ἅπασα, ἅπαν, adj. all together

ἀπ-αυθαδίζομαι, v.d.i. be very arrogant

ἀ-πειθέω, v.i. disobey (with dat.)

ἄπ-ειμι, v.i., impf. ἀπῇα, partic. ἀπιών, go away

ἄ-πειρ-ος, -ον, adj. inexperienced in, unused to (with gen.)

ἀπ-ελαύνω, v.t. (for parts see ἐξελαύνω), drive away

ἀπ-εχθάνομαι, v.d.i., fut. -εχθήσομαι, aor. -ηχθόμην, pf. -ήχθημαι, incur hatred, become hateful to (with dat.)

ἀπέχθει-α ἡ, -ας, hatred, enmity

ἀ-πιστέω, v.i. disbelieve; be unconvinced

ἄ-πιστ-ος, -ον, adj.
    (1) *not believed in, uncon-vincing*
    (2) *not believing, distrustful*

ἀπό, prep. with gen., *from, away from*

ἀπο-βαίνω, v.i. (for parts see ἀναβαίνω), *go away*; *result from*

ἀπο-δείκνυμι, v.t. *show, ex-plain, prove*

ἀπο-δημέω, v.i. *be away from one's people, travel abroad*

ἀπο-δημί-α ἡ, -ας, *sojourn abroad*

ἀπο-θνήσκω, v.i. *die, be killed*

ἀπο-κρίνομαι, v.d.i. *answer* (with dat.)

ἀπο-κρύπτω, v.t. *hide away, conceal*

ἀπο-κτείνω, v.t., inf. -κτεινύναι and -κτείνειν, fut. -κτενῶ, aor. ἀπέκτεινα, pf. ἀπέκτονα, *kill, put to death*

ἀπο-λαύω, v.i. fut. -λαύσομαι, *enjoy*; *derive gain from* (with gen.)

ἀπο-λείπω, v.t. *desert*

Ἀπολλόδωρ-ος ὁ, -ου, *Apollodorus*

ἀπ-όλλυμι, v.t., fut. -ολῶ, aor. -ώλεσα, pf. -ολώλεκα, *destroy*; mid. and str. pf. -όλωλα, aor. -ωλόμην, *perish*

ἀπολογέομαι, v.d.i. *defend oneself*; verbal neut. adj. ἀπ-λογητέον, *defence must be made*

ἀπο-λογί-α ἡ, -ας, *defence*

ἀπο-λύω, v.t. *loose from*; mid. *do away with*

ἀπο-πειράομαι, v.d.i. *make trial of* (with gen.); *test*

ἀ-πορέω, v.i. *be in difficulties; be at a loss*

ἄ-πορ-ος, -ον, adj. *difficult to deal with, impracticable*

ἀπο-τίνω, v.t. *pay back*; *pay a fine*

ἀπο-τρέπω, v.t. *turn away from*

ἀπο-φαίνω, v.t. *make known*; *explain*

ἀπο-φεύγω, v.i. *flee away, be acquitted*

ἀπο-ψηφίζομαι, v.d.i. *vote in acquittal, acquit*

ἆρα, particle introducing questions; Lat. *-ne?*

ἄρα, particle, *then; as it seems, after all; indeed*

ἀργύρι-ον τό, -ου, *silver; money*

ἀρετ-ή ἡ, -ῆς, *virtue, excellence*

ἀριθμ-ός ὁ, -οῦ, *number*

Ἀριστοφάν-ης ὁ, -ους, *Aristophanes*

Ἀρίστ-ων ὁ, -ωνος, *Ariston*

ἄρουρ-α ἡ, -ας (Homeric -η, -ης), *soil, ground*

ἄρτι, adv. *just now, lately*

ἀρχ-ή ἡ, -ῆς, *beginning*; *public office*; *government*; τὴν ἀρχήν, adverbial, *at all*

ἄρχω, v.i. *rule* (with gen.); act. and mid. *begin* (with gen.)

ἄρχ-ων ὁ, -οντος, *ruler; cap-tain; official*

ἀ-σέβει-α ἡ, -ας, *impiety*

ἀσπάζομαι, v.d.t. *salute, greet*

ἀστ-ός ὁ, -οῦ, *fellow-citizen*

ἀ-σχολί-α ἡ, -ας, *lack of leisure; occupation;* ἀσχολίαν ἄγειν, *be busy*

ἄτε, conj. *inasmuch as* (with partic.)

ἀτεχνῶς, adv. *literally, altogether*

ἀ-τιμάζω, v.t. *dishonour, despise*

ἀ-τιμόω, v.t. *dishonour; disfranchise*

ἄ-τοπ-ος, -ον, adj. *out of the way, strange*

ἄττα, n. plur. nom. voc. acc. of τις

αὖ, adv. *again; on the other hand*

αὐθάδ-ης, -ες, adj. *stubborn, hard-hearted*

αὐθαδίζομαι, v.d.i. *be self-willed, be arrogant*

αὖθις, adv. *again, hereafter*

αὐλητ-ής ὁ, -οῦ, *flute-player*

αὐλητικ-ός, -ή, -όν, adj. *concerned with flutes*

αὐτίκα, adv. *at once, immediately*

αὐτόθι, adv. *there*

αὐτό-ματ-ος, -η, -ον, adj. *of one's own accord, spontaneous.* ἀπὸ τοῦ αὐτομάτου, *in the course of nature; by chance*

αὐτ-όν, -οῦ, contracted for ἑαυτόν

αὐτός, contracted for ὁ αὐτός

αὐτ-ός, -ή, -ό, pron. *self, in person;* in oblique cases, *he, she, it,* etc.; ὁ αὐτός, *the same*

αὐτο-σχεδιάζω, v.i. *speak out of one's head, off-hand; extemporise*

αὐτό-φωρ-ος, -ον, adj. *in the act of thieving*

ἀ-φθονί-α ἡ, -ας, *freedom from envy, abundance*

ἀφ-ίημι, v.t., fut. -ήσω, aor. -ῆκα, *send away; let go; throw away; acquit*

ἀφ-ικνέομαι, v.d.i. fut. -ίξομαι, aor. -ικόμην, pf. -ῖγμαι, *arrive*

ἄχθομαι, v.d.i., fut. ἀχθέσομαι, aor. ἠχθέσθην, pf. ἤχθημαι, *be grieved; be angry* (with dat.)

ἄχθ-ος τό, -ους, *burden, cumberer*

βαρ-ύς, -εῖα, -ύ, adj. *heavy; grievous; irksome*

βασιλ-εύς ὁ, -έως, *king*

βελτίων. See ἀγαθός

βιάζομαι, v.d.t. *overpower; prevail on*

βιβλί-ον τό, -ου, *book*

βί-ος, ὁ, -ου, *life*

βιόω, v.i., fut. βιώσομαι, *live*

βιωτ-ός, -όν, adj. *to be lived, worth living*

βλαβερ-ός, -ά, -όν, adj. *harmful*

βλάπτω, v.t., fut. βλάψω, str. aor. pass. ἐβλάβην, *harm, injure*

βοάω, v.i., fut. βοήσομαι. *cry out; make disturbance*

βοηθέω, v.i. *help* (with dat.)

βουλευτ-ής ὁ, -οῦ, *member of the Council; councillor*

βουλεύω, v.t. and i. *counsel, be a member of the Council* (at Athens); also v.d. βουλεύομαι

βούλομαι, v.d.t., fut. βουλή-
σομαι, wish

βραδ-ύς, -εῖα, -ύ, adj. slow

γάρ, conj. for; καὶ γάρ, for
indeed, for also; ἀλλὰ γάρ,
but in point of fact, but in
truth

γε, particle, at least, at any
rate; yes; γε δέ, yes and

γελοῖ-ος, -α, -ον, adj. laugh-
able; quaint

γέμω, v.i. be full of (with
gen.)

γενναῖ-ος, -α, -ον, adj. noble

γέν-ος τό, -ους, race

γεωργικ-ός, -ή, -όν, adj.
skilled in farming

γῆ ἡ, γῆς, earth

γίγνομαι, v.d.i., fut. γενή-
σομαι, aor. ἐγενόμην, pf.
γέγονα and γεγένημαι,
become, happen; pf. partic.
γεγονώς, aged

γιγνώσκω, v.t., fut. γνώ-
σομαι, aor. ἔγνων, pf.
ἔγνωκα, observe, know

γνησίως, adv. genuinely;
honestly

Γοργί-ας ὁ, -ου, Gorgias

γοῦν, particle, at any rate

γράμμα τό, -τος, writing;
letter; plur. letters, literature

γραφ-ή ἡ, -ῆς, drawing, writing, indictment

γράφω, v.t. and i. write; mid.
indict

γυνή ἡ, gen. γυναικός, woman

δαιμόνι-ος, -α, -ον, adj.
divine, supernatural; as noun

δαιμόνι-ον, divinity; the
'divine sign' of Socrates

δαίμ-ων ὁ, ἡ, -ονος, divine being

δάκρυ-ον τό, -ου, tear

δέ, conj. but, and, now; on the
other hand (answering to μέν)

δ' οὖν, particle, anyhow, at all
events

δεῖ, v. impers., fut. δεήσει, it
is necessary

δείδω, v.i., fut. δείσω, aor.
ἔδεισα (also pf. with pres.
meaning δέδοικα and
δέδια), fear

δείκνυμι, v.t., fut. δείξω, aor.
ἔδειξα, show, point out

δειν-ός, -ή, -όν, adj. terrible,
strange, monstrous, clever;
δεινὸς λέγειν, clever at
speaking

δέκα, numerical adj., indecl.
ten

Δελφ-οί οἱ, -ῶν, Delphi

δεσμ-ός ὁ, -οῦ, bonds, imprisonment

δεσμωτήρι-ον τό, -ου, prison

δεῦρο, adv. hither; come here

δέχομαι, v.d.t. receive, accept;
consent

δέω (1), v.i., fut. δεήσω, lack;
be far from; mid. want, need;
beg, request (with gen.)
(2), v.t. bind; pass. (pf.
δέδεμαι), be in prison

δή, particle, indeed, so, wherefore, generally for emphasis

Δήλι-ον τό, -ου, Delium

δῆλ-ος, -η, -ον, adj. plain,
manifest

δημηγορί-α ἡ, -ας, public
speaking

107

δημιουργ-ός ὁ, -οῦ, craftsman

Δημόδοκ-ος ὁ, -ου, Demodocus

δημοκρατέομαι, v.d.i. have a democratic constitution

δημοσιεύω, v.i. be a public man

δημόσι-ος, -α, -ον, adj. public; dat. fem. as adv. δημοσίᾳ, publicly

δημότ-ης ὁ, -ου, of the same deme in Attica

δήπου, particle, I suppose, of course

δῆτα, adv. surely; then

διά, prep.
(1) with acc. owing to, because of
(2) with gen. through (of place or time); by means of

Δία, acc. of Ζεύς, Zeus

δια-βάλλω, v.t., fut. -βαλῶ, aor. διέβαλον, pf. -βέβληκα, slander, calumniate

δια-βολ-ή ἡ, -ῆς, prejudice; scandal

δια-γίγνομαι, v.d.t. live through

δι-άγω, v.t. and i. pass the time: live

δια-κινδυνεύω, v.i. run a great risk

δια-κωλύω, v.t. hinder

δια-λέγομαι, v.d.i., pf. διείλεγμαι, converse (with dat.)

δια-μυθολογέω, v.i. interchange one's fancies

δια-νοέομαι, v.d.t. intend; think

διάνοι-α ἡ, -ας, thought, intention

δια-πειράομαι, v.d.i. try an experiment (with gen.)

δια-σκοπέω, v.t. examine thoroughly

δια-τελέω, v.i., fut. -τελῶ, continue

δια-τριβ-ή ἡ, -ῆς, mode of life, study

δια-τρίβω, v.i. spend time; employ oneself

δια-φέρω, v.t. and i. bear through; (with gen.) be different from, excel

δια-φεύγω, v.i. escape; get off

δια-φθείρω, v.t., fut. διαφθερῶ, aor. διέφθειρα, pf. διέφθαρκα, corrupt

διδάσκαλ-ος ὁ, -ου, master

διδάσκω, v.t. teach; mid. get oneself taught, learn

δίδωμι, v.t., fut. δώσω, aor. ἔδωκα, pf. δέδωκα, pf. pass. δέδομαι, give, pay

δι-ερωτάω, v.t. cross-question, question constantly

διθύραμβ-ος ὁ, -ου, dithyrambic hymn

δικάζω, v.i. give judgment

δίκαι-ος, -α, -ον, adj. just, righteous; adv. δικαίως

δικαστήρι-ον τό, -ου, court of justice

δικαστ-ής ὁ, -οῦ, judge, juryman

δίκ-η ἡ, -ης, justice; suit at law; penalty

δι-όμνυμι, v.t. swear solemnly

διττ-ός, -ή, -όν, adj. twofold, of two kinds

διώκω, v.t. pursue, prosecute

108

δοκέω, v.t. and i., fut. δόξω, *think*; intrans. *seem*; impers. **δοκεῖ**, *it seems; it seems good*; **ἔδοξε**, *it seemed good, it was resolved*

δόξ-α ἡ, -ης, *opinion; reputation; glory*

δόσ-ις ἡ, -εως, *gift*

δουλεύω, v.i. *be a slave to, serve* (with dat.)

δρᾶμα τό, -τος, *doing; drama scene*

δραχμ-ή ἡ, -ῆς, *drachma, a silver coin, worth about* 9½*d.*

δρῦς ἡ, δρυός, *oak*

δύναμαι, v.d.i., fut. δυνή-σομαι, aor. ἐδυνήθην, *be able*

δυνατ-ός, -ή, -όν, adj. *able, possible*

δύο, δυοῖν, numerical adj. *two*

δυστυχί-α ἡ, -ας, *misfortune*

ἐάν, conj. *if* (with subj.)

ἐάν-περ, conj. *if in truth*

ἐαυτ-όν, -ήν, -ό, pron. (no nom.) *himself*

ἐάω, v.t., fut. ἐάσω, aor. εἴασα, pf. εἴακα, *allow, leave alone, overlook*

ἑβδομήκοντα, numerical adj., indecl. *seventy*

ἐγγυάομαι, v.d.i. *stand surety* (with dat.)

ἐγγυητ-ής ὁ, -οῦ, *surety*

ἐγγύς, adv. and prep. with gen., comp. ἐγγυτέρω, superl. ἐγγυτάτω or ἐγγύτατα, *nearly; near*

ἐγείρω, v.t., fut. ἐγερῶ, aor.

ἤγειρα, *rouse, wake up*; str. pf. ἐγρήγορα, *be awake*

ἐγ-καλέω, v.t. and i. *bring a charge against, accuse of* (with acc. of crime, dat. of pers.)

ἔγκλημα τό, -τος, *accusation, charge*

ἐγώ, pron. ἐμοῦ, or μου, *I.* **ἔγωγε** = ἐγώ γε, emphatic, *I, for my part; I indeed*

ἐθέλω, or **θέλω**, v.i., aor. ἠθέλησα or ἐθέλησα, *be willing*

ἐθίζω, v.t., pf. pass. εἴθισμαι, *accustom*; mid. *accustom oneself*

εἰ, conj. *if* (with ind. or opt.); εἰ δὲ μή, *but failing that*

εἰδέναι, inf. of **οἶδα**

εἶεν, interj. *well!*

εἰκῆ, adv. *at random*

εἷλον, aor. of **αἱρέω**

εἰμί, v. aux. and i., fut. ἔσομαι, *be*

εἶμι, v.i. *go; will go*

εἴ-περ, conj. *if actually*

εἶπον, used as aor. of **φημί**

εἴρηκα, used as pf. of **φημί**

εἰρωνεύομαι, v.d.i. *talk ironically, be insincere*

εἰς, prep. with acc. *into, to; against*

εἷς, μία, ἕν, numerical adj. *one*

εἰσ-άγω, v.t. *bring into; bring to trial*

εἴσ-ειμι, v.i. *will go into*

εἶτα, adv. *then, next*

εἴωθα, pf. with pres. meaning, *am accustomed*

ἐκ or ἐξ, prep. with gen., *out of, from*

ἕκαστ-ος, -η, -ον, adj. *each*

ἑκάστοτε, adv. *on each occasion, always*

ἑκάτερ-ος, -α, -ον, adj. *each of two; pl. each set of two*

ἐκεῖ, adv. *there yonder; in the other world*

ἐκεῖν-ος, -η, -ο, pron. and adj. *that, yonder; he, she, it;* adv. ἐκείνως, *in that way*

ἐκκλησί-α ἡ, -ας, *Assembly* (at Athens)

ἐκκλησιαστ-ής ὁ, -οῦ, *member of the Assembly*

ἐκ-λέγω, v.t. *pick out*

ἐκ-πλήττω, v.t. *dismay*

ἐκ-τίνω, v.t. *pay off*

Ἕκτ-ωρ ὁ, -ορος, *Hector*

ἐκ-φεύγω, v.t. *escape from*

ἐκ-ών, -οῦσα, -όν, adj. *willing*

ἐλάττ-ων, -ον, comp. adj. *less;* superl. ἐλάχιστος, *least*

ἔλεγχ-ος ὁ, -ου, *proof; account*

ἐλέγχω, v.t. *cross-question, test, confute*

ἐλεειν-ός, -ή, -όν, adj. *pitiful, wretched*

ἐλεέω, v.t. *pity;* pass. *be pitied, excite compassion*

ἐλπ-ίς ἡ, -ίδος, *hope*

ἐμαυτ-όν, -ήν, pron. *myself*

ἐμμελῶς, adv. *harmoniously, moderately*

ἐμ-μένω, v.i. *abide by* (with dat.)

ἐμ-ός, -ή, -όν, poss. adj. *my*

ἐμ-πίπλημι, v.t. (for parts see ἀναπίμπλημι), *fill full; din into*

ἐμ-πνέω, v.i. *breathe; live*

ἔμπροσθεν, adv. *before*

ἐν, prep. with dat., *in, within; among;* ἐν ᾧ, *while*

ἐναντιόομαι, v.d.i. *oppose, forbid* (with dat.)

ἐν-αντί-ος, -α, -ον, adj. *opposite, opposed to;* τοὐναν-τίον, adv. *on the contrary*

ἐνδε-ής, -ές, adj. *wanting, in need of* (with gen.)

ἐν-δείκνυμι, v.t. *point out;* mid. *give proof*

ἔνδεκα, numerical adj. indecl. *eleven*

ἕνεκα, prep. with gen. *on account of, for the sake of*

ἐνθάδε, adv. *here*

ἐνθένδε, adv. *hence*

ἐνθουσιάζω, v.i. *be inspired; be enthusiastic*

ἐν-θυμέομαι, v.d.t. *lay to heart; ponder*

ἔνι-οι, -αι, -α, plur. adj. *some*

ἐνίοτε, adv. *sometimes, occasionally*

ἐν-νοέω, v.t. *reflect on, bear in mind*

ἐνταῦθα, adv. *here, there*

ἐνταυθοῖ, adv. *hither*

ἐντεῦθεν, adv. *thence, thereupon*

ἐν-τυγχάνω, v.i. *fall in with; meet* (with dat.)

ἐν-ύπνι-ον τό, -ου, *vision in sleep, dream*

ἐξ-αιρέω, v.i. with gen. *take out, choose out*

ἐξ-αμαρτάνω, v.i., fut.
-αμαρτήσομαι, aor. -ήμαρτον,
pf. -ημάρτηκα, err grievously;
fail

ἐξαπατάω, v.t. deceive, mis-
lead completely

ἔξ-ειμι, v.i. go out

ἐξ-ελαύνω, v.t., fut. -ελῶ,
aor. -ήλασα, pf. -ελήλακα,
drive away; banish

ἐξ-ελέγχω, v.t. convict, confute

ἐξ-εργάζομαι, v.d.t. bring to
perfection, be very skilful in

ἐξ-έρχομαι, v.d.i. come out or
go out

ἔξεστι, v. impers. it is allowed, it is possible

ἐξ-ετάζω, v.t. examine closely

ἐξ-έτασ-ις ἡ, -εως, enquiry,
examination

ἐξ-ευρίσκω, v.t. discover

ἔοικα, pf. with pres. meaning,
be like, seem

ἐπ-αΐω, v.t. understand, be
professor of

ἐπ-ακολουθέω, v.i. follow
after (with dat.)

ἐπεί, conj. when, since; and yet

ἐπειδάν, conj. = ἐπειδὴ ἄν,
whenever, so soon as

ἐπειδή, conj. when, since

ἐπειδή-περ, conj. since as you
say

ἔπειτα, adv. then, next

ἐπ-έχω, v.t. hold back,
restrain

ἐπί, prep.

(1) with acc. to, towards,
against; with a view to

(2) with gen. upon, at

(3) with dat. upon; at (of
price), in the power of; with a
view to; following

ἐφ' ᾧτε, on condition that

Ἐπιγέν-ης ὁ, -ους, Epigenes

ἐπι-δείκνυμι, v.t. set forth;
display

ἐπι-δημέω, v.i. reside here (of
foreigners)

ἐπιεικ-ής, -ές, adj. good, well
fitted

ἐπι-θυμέω, v.i. desire (with
gen.)

ἐπι-κωμῳδέω, v.i. make mock
(as in a comedy)

ἐπι-λανθάνομαι, v.d.i.
forget (with gen.)

ἐπι-μελοῦμαι, v.d.i. care for;
look after (with gen.)

ἐπι-ορκέω, v.i. commit perjury

ἐπι-πέμπω, v.t. send upon

ἐπίσταμαι, v.d.t. know

ἐπιστάτ-ης ὁ, -ου, master,
trainer; president

ἐπιστήμ-η ἡ, -ης, knowledge

ἐπιστήμ-ων, -ον, adj.
knowing, learned in (with
gen.)

ἐπιτήδευμα τό, -τος, occupation

ἐπιτηδεύω, v.t. be occupied
with; practise

ἐπι-τίθημι, v.t. place upon;
impose, inflict; mid. ἐπιτίθ-
εμαι, fut. ἐπιθήσομαι, aor.
ἐπεθέμην, set upon, attack

ἐπι-τρέπω, v.t. entrust;
permit

ἐπι-τυγχάνω, v.i. meet with
(with dat.); aor. partic. ὁ
ἐπιτυχών, the first that comes

ἐπί-φθον-ος, -ον, adj.
  odious, objectionable
ἐπι-χειρέω, v.i. *put one's
  hand to, attempt*
ἐπι-χειρητέον, verbal neut.
  adj. *attempt must be made*
ἐπ-ονείδιστ-ος, -ον, adj.
  worthy of reproach, shameful
ἔπ-ος τό, -ους, *word*
ἐργάζομαι, v.d.t., pf. εἴργα-
  σμαι, *do; produce*
ἔργ-ον τό, -ου, *work, deed*; in
  dat. ἔργῳ, *in fact, actually*
ἐρευνάω, v.t. *search after,
  investigate, examine*
ἔρημ-ος, -η, -ον, adj. *de-
  serted*; ἐρήμη (supply δίκη),
  an undefended action at law
ἔρομαι, v.d., fut. ἐρήσομαι, *ask*
ἔρχομαι, v.d.i., fut. εἶμι,
  aor. ἦλθον, pf. ἐλήλυθα,
  come, go
ἐρῶ, used as fut. of φημί
ἐρωτάω, v.t. *ask*
ἔσχατ-ος, -η, -ον, adj. *last,
  extreme*
ἑταῖρ-ος ὁ, -ου, *companion*
ἕτερ-ος, -α, -ον, adj. *the
  other, one of two*
ἔτι, adv. *yet, still*
ἑτοῖμ-ος, -ον, adj. *ready, pre-
  pared*
ἔτ-ος τό, -ους, *year*
εὖ, adv. *well*
εὐ-αρίθμητ-ος, -ον, *easily
  numbered; few*
εὐ-δαιμονί-α ἡ, -ας, *happiness; good fortune*
εὐ-δαίμ-ων, -ον, adj. *happy*
εὐ-δοκιμέω, v.i. *be of good
  repute*

εὐ-δόκιμ-ος, -ον, adj. *renowned*
εὐ-έλεγκτ-ος, -ον, adj. *easily
  proved*
εὔ-ελπ-ις, -ι, adj. *of good
  hope*
εὐ-εργεσί-α ἡ, -ας, *kind
  deed*
εὐ-εργετέω, v.i. *do a kindness*
  (with cognate acc.)
Εὔην-ος ὁ, -ον, *Evenus*
εὐθύς, adv. *immediately*
εὐλαβέομαι, v.d.t. *beware, be
  careful*
εὑρίσκω, v.t., fut. εὑρήσω,
  aor. εὖρον, pf. εὕρηκα, *find*
εὐ-σεβέω, v.i. *be pious, act
  righteously*
ἐφεξῆς, adv. *successively, one
  after another*
ἔφησθα, 2 pers. sing. impf.
  from φημί
ἔχω, v.t., fut. ἕξω or σχήσω,
  aor. ἔσχον (inf. σχεῖν), pf.
  ἔσχηκα, *hold, have*; v.i. (with
  inf.) *be able; hold oneself, be*
  (especially with adverbs, as
  οὕτως ἔχει, *it is so*;
  ξένως ἔχω, *I am a
  stranger to*); mid. *cling to*
ἔωθεν, adv. *early in the
  morning*
ἕως, conj. *so long as, until*
ἕωσπερ, conj. *so long as ever*

ζάω (ζῇς, ζῇ, 2 pers. plur.
  ζῆτε), inf. ζῆν, v.i. *live*
ζεῦγ-ος τό, -ους, *team of four
  horses*
Ζεύς ὁ, gen. Διός, *Zeus*
ζητέω, v.t. *seek; examine*

ζήτησ-ις ἡ, -εως, *search*

ζῷ-ον τό, -ου, *animal*

ἤ, conj. *either, or; than*

ἤ, particle, introducing a question. ἤ μήν, particle of asseveration, *yea verily*

ᾖα, impf. of εἶμι

ἡβάω, v.i. *grow up*

ἡγέομαι, v.d.t. and i. *lead; think, suppose*

ἡδέως, adv. of ἡδύς, *gladly*; comp. ἤδιον, superl. ἤδιστα

ἤδη, adv. *already, by this time, now*

ἡδ-ύς, -εῖα, -ύ, adj. *sweet, pleasant*; comp. ἡδίων, superl. ἤδιστος

ἤκ-ω, v.i. *have come*; fut. ἤξω, *will come*

Ἠλεῖος, adj. *of Elis*

ἡλικί-α ἡ, -ας, *age, time of life*

ἡλικιώτ-ης ὁ, -οῦ, *contemporary*

ἥλι-ος ὁ, -ου, *sun*

ἡμ-εῖς, pron. -ῶν, *we*

ἡμέρ-α ἡ, -ας, *day*

ἡμί-θε-ος ὁ, -ου, *demi-god, hero*

ἡμί-ον-ος ὁ, -ου, *half-donkey, mule*

ἦν (1) impf. of εἰμί
(2) impf. of ἠμί, *say*

ἡνίκα, conj. *when*

Ἥρ-α ἡ, -ας, *Hera*

ἥρως ὁ, ἥρωος and ἥρω, *hero*

Ἡσίοδ-ος ὁ, -ου, *Hesiod*

ἡσυχί-α ἡ, -ας, *rest, quiet*; ἡσυχίαν ἄγω, *keep quiet*

ἤ-τοι, conj. *either indeed*

ἤττ-ων, -ον, comp. adj. *less, weaker, worse*, superl. ἥκιστος

θάνατ-ος ὁ, -ου, *death*

θαρραλέως, adv. *undauntedly*; θαρραλέως ἔχω, *be of good cheer*

θάτερ-ον τό, -ου, for τὸ ἕτερον, *one thing of two*

θάττ-ων, -ον, comp. of ταχύς; adv. θᾶττον

θαυμάζω, v.t. *admire, wonder*

θαυμάσι-ος, -α, -ον, adj. *wonderful, astonishing*

θαυμαστ-ός, -ή, -όν, adj. *wonderful, marvellous*

Θεάγ-ης ὁ, -ου, *Theages*

θεῖ-ος, -α, -ον, adj. *godlike, divine*

θέλω, see ἐθέλω

θέμ-ις ἡ, , -ιτος *right, law*

θεμιτ-ός, -ή, -όν, adj. *lawful, righteous*

Θεόδοτ-ος ὁ, -ου, *Theodotus*

Θεοζοτίδ-ης ὁ, -ου, *Theozotides*

θεό-μαντ-ις ὁ, -εως, *prophet of the god, soothsayer*

θε-ός ὁ, -οῦ, *god*

Θέτ-ις ἡ, -ιδος, *Thetis*

θέω, v.i. *run*

θνήσκω, v.i., fut. θανοῦμαι, aor. ἔθανον, pf. τέθνηκα (str. pf. opt. τεθναίην, inf. τεθνάναι, partic. τεθνεώς), *die*

θόλ-ος ἡ, -ου, *dome; Rotunda*

θορυβέω, v.i. *make a disturbance, interrupt*

θρηνέω, v.i. *lament*

ἴδι-ος, -α, -ον, adj. *one's own; private*; dat. fem. as adv. ἰδίᾳ, *privately*

ἰδιωτεύω, v.i. *live a private life*

ἰδιώτ-ης ὁ, -ου, *private person*

ἴθι, ἴτω imper. of εἶμι

ἱκαν-ός, -ή, -όν, adj. *enough, sufficient*; adv. ἱκανῶς

ἱκετεί-α ἡ, -ας, *supplication*

ἱκετεύω, v.t. *supplicate*

ἵνα, conj. *in order that* (with subj. or opt.); *where*

Ἱππί-ας ὁ, -ου, *Hippias*

ἱππικ-ός, -ή, -όν, adj. *who understands horses; concerned with horses*

Ἱππόνικ-ος ὁ, -ου, *Hipponicus*

ἵππ-ος ὁ, ἡ, -ου, *horse*

ἴσ-μεν, -τε, -ασι, plur. of οἶδα

ἵστημι, v.t. and i., fut. στήσω, wk. aor. ἔστησα, *make to stand, place, set up*; mid. with str. aor. ἔστην, and pf. ἔστηκα, *stand, halt, stop*

ἰσχυρ-ός, -ά, -όν, adj. *strong*

ἰσχ-ύς ἡ, -ύος, *strength*

ἴσως, adv. *perhaps*

ἰτέον, verbal neut. adj. from εἶμι, *one must go*

ἰών, partic. of εἶμι

καθεύδω, v.i. *sleep*

κάθημαι, v.d.i. *sit*

καθ-ίστημι, v.t. and i., fut. καταστήσω, wk. aor. κατέστησα, *place, appoint; bring into*; mid., str. aor. κατέ-στην, and pf. καθέστηκα, *place oneself, stand; enter on; exist*

καί, conj. *and; also, too; even, actually*; καί—καί or τε—καί, *both—and*; καὶ δὴ καί, *and especially*

καιν-ός, -ή, -όν, adj. *new*

καί-περ, conj. *although*

κακί-α ἡ, -ας, *wickedness*

κακ-ός, -ή, -όν, adj. *bad, cowardly*

καλέω, v.t., fut. καλέσω or καλῶ, aor. ἐκάλεσα, pf. κέ-κληκα, *call*

Καλλί-ας ὁ, -ου, *Callias*

καλλιεπέομαι, v.d.i., pf. κεκαλλιέπημαι with pass. meaning, *say in fine words, ornament*

καλλύνω, v.t. *beautify*; mid. *pride oneself in*

καλ-ός, -ή, -όν, adj. *beautiful, noble*; καλός τε κἀγαθός, *excellent, of perfect breeding*; comp. καλλίων, superl. κάλλιστος

καλ-ῶς, adv. *well*

κατά, prep. (1) with acc., *down, over, along; according to* (2) with gen., *down over; down from; against*

κατα-γέλαστ-ος, -ον, adj. *laughed to scorn; a laughing-stock*

κατα-γελάω, v.i., fut. -γελά-σομαι (with gen.), *laugh to scorn*

κατα-γιγνώσκω, v.t. *discover (a weakness); accuse;*

VOCABULARY

condemn (with acc. of the crime, gen. of person)

κατα-δαρθάνω, v.i., aor. κατέδαρθον, *fall asleep*; *be asleep*

κατα-δέομαι, v.d.i. *entreat earnestly* (with gen.)

κατά-δηλ-ος, -ον, adj. *quite plain*; *detected*

κατα-λαμβάνω, v.t. *seize upon*

κατα-λύω, v.t. *put an end to, abolish*

κατα-νοέω, v.t. *perceive, understand*

κατα-σκεδάννυμι, v.t., fut. -σκεδάσω, *scatter about, spread abroad*

κατα-φρονέω, v.i. *look down upon, despise* (with gen.)

κατα-χαρίζομαι, v.d.t. *wrongly make a present of; bestow by favour*

κατα-ψηφίζομαι, v.d.t., fut. -ψηφιοῦμαι, *vote against; condemn* (with acc. of sentence, gen. of pers.)

κατ-έρχομαι, v.d. *come back; return from exile*

κατ-έχω, v.t. *hold in check*

κατηγορέω, v.i. *accuse* (with gen.)

κατηγορί-α ἡ, -ας, *accusation*

κατήγορ-ος ὁ, -ον, *accuser*

Κεῖος, adj. *of Ceos*

κελεύω, v.t. *command, bid*

κέρδ-ος τό, -ους, *gain*

κήδομαι, v.d. *be concerned for; take an interest in* (with gen.)

Κηφισιεύς, adj. *belonging to the deme Cephisia*

κινδυνεύω, v.i. *be in danger of*; *seem*

κίνδυν-ος ὁ, -ου, *danger*

Κλαζομέν-ι-ος, -α, -ον, adj. *of Clazomenae*

κόλασ-ις ἡ, -εως, *punishment*

κολούω, v.t. *cut short, suppress*

κορων-ίς, -ίδος, adj. *beaked*

κοσμέω, v.t. *adorn*

κρείττ-ων, -ον, comp. adj. *stronger, better*

κρίνω, v.t. *judge*

κρίσ-ις ἡ, -εως, *judgement, condemnation*

Κριτόβουλ-ος ὁ, -ου, *Critobulus*

Κρίτ-ων ὁ, -ωνος, *Crito*

κρούω, v.t. *knock, crush*

κτάω, v.t. *acquire*; mid. *possess*

κτῆσ-ις ἡ, -εως, *possession*

κύων ὁ, ἡ, κυνός, *dog*

κωλύω, v.t. *hinder*

κωμῳδί-α ἡ, -ας, *comedy*

κωμῳδοποι-ός ὁ, -οῦ, *writer of comedies*

λαμβάνω, v.t., fut. λήψομαι, aor. ἔλαβον, pf. εἴληφα, *take, seize; receive*

λανθάνω, v.t. and i., fut. λήσομαι, aor. ἔλαθον, pf. λέληθα, *escape notice*

λατρεί-α ἡ, -ας, *service; devotion, worship*

λέγω, v.t. *say, speak, mean*

λείπω, v.t., fut. λείψω, aor. ἔλιπον, pf. λέλοιπα, *leave; desert*

λέξ-ις ἡ, -εως, *style* (of speech)

Λεοντῖνος, adj. *of Leontini*

Λέ-ων ὁ, -οντος, *Leon*

λίθ-ος ὁ, -ου, *stone*

λογίζομαι, v.d.t., fut. λογιοῦμαι, aor. ἐλογισάμην, pf. λελόγισμαι, *reckon, consider*

λόγ-ος ὁ, -ου, *word; speech; talk; argument; cause*

λοιδορέω, v.t. *abuse, revile*

λοιπ-ός, -ή, -όν, adj. *remaining*

Λύκ-ων ὁ, -ωνος, *Lycon*

λυπέω, v.t. *grieve, pain;* pass. *be pained*

Λυσανί-ας ὁ, -ου, *Lysanias*

λυσιτελέω, v.i. *profit;* usually impers. with dat. λυσιτελεῖ, *it is profitable, it is better*

μά, particle, *by* (in oaths, negative)

μάθημα τό, -τος, *learning, knowledge*

μάθησ-ις ἡ, -εως, *instruction*

μαθητ-ής ὁ, -οῦ, *disciple*

μακαρίζω, v.t. *think happy, fortunate*

μάλα, adv. *much, greatly;* comp. μᾶλλον, *more, rather;* superl. μάλιστα, *most; about* (in round numbers); (in answers) *certainly*

μανθάνω, v.t. and i., fut. μαθήσομαι, aor. ἔμαθον, pf. μεμάθηκα, *learn, find out, understand*

μαντεί-α ἡ, -as, *prophecy, oracle*

μαντεῖ-ον τό, -ου, *oracle*

μαντεύομαι, v.d.t. *divine, foretell; enquire of an oracle*

μαντικ-ή ἡ, -ῆς, *art of divination*

μαρτυρέω, v.i. *bear witness*

μάρτ-υς ὁ, -υρος, *witness*

μάχ-η, ἡ, -ης, *battle*

μάχομαι, v.d.i., fut. μαχοῦμαι, aor. ἐμαχεσάμην, pf. μεμάχημαι, *fight*

μέγας, μεγάλη, μέγα, adj. *great, important;* comp. μείζων, superl. μέγιστος

μέγεθ-ος τό, -ους, *size; great size*

μειράκι-ον τό, -ου, *lad, stripling*

Μέλητ-ος ὁ, -ου, *Meletus*

μέλλω, v.i. *be about to be; be likely to be*

μέλω, v.i., fut. μελήσω, *be a care* (with dat.); impers. μέλει, *it is a care;* partic. μέλον

μέμφομαι, v.d.t. *blame* (with acc. of pers., or acc. of thing and dat. of pers.)

μέν, particle, *indeed; on the one hand,* answered by δέ

μὲν οὖν, particle, *so then; nay rather*

μέν-τοι, conj. *however; yes, to be sure, indeed*

μένω, v.t. and i., *wait for; remain*

μέρ-ος τό, -ους, *share, part*

μετά, prep.
    (1) with acc., *after*
    (2) with gen., *with*

μεταβολ-ή ἡ, -ῆς, *change*

μετα-λαμβάνω, v.t. *obtain a share of* (with share in acc.)

μετα-μέλει, v. impers. with dat. *repent*; μεταμέλει μοι, *it repents me, I repent*

μεταξύ, adv. *between; in the middle of*

μετα-πέμπω, v.t. *send for* (so also in mid.)

μετα-πίπτω, v.i., fut. -πεσοῦμαι, aor. μετέπεσον, pf. -πέπτωκα, *fall the other way, change sides*

μέτ-ειμι, v.i. *be among*; impers. μέτεστί μοι, *I have a share in* (with share in nom.)

μετέωρ-ος, -ον, adj. *in the air*

μετοίκησ-ις ἡ, -εως, *change of dwelling, migration*

μετρίως, adv. *in due measure*; μετρίως ἔχει, *it is well*

μή, neg. particle, *not; do not; lest*, after verbs of fearing, etc.

μηδαμῶς, adv. *by no means*

μηδέ, neg. conj. *nor; not even*

μηδ-είς, μηδεμία, μηδέν, numerical adj. *none, no one*

μηκέτι, adv. *no longer*

μήν, particle, *truly*

μηνύω, v.t. *indicate; inform against; disclose*

μή-τε, neg. conj. *neither, nor*

μήτηρ ἡ, μητρός, *mother*

μηχανάομαι, v.d.t. *contrive, manœuvre*

μηχαν-ή ἡ, -ῆς, *instrument; means, way*

μιαρ-ός, -ά, -όν, adj. *abominable*

μικρ-ός, -ά, -όν, adj. *little, small*

μιμέομαι, v.d.t. *imitate; mimic*

μιμνήσκω, v.t. *remind*; mid. pf. in pres. sense, μέμνημαι, fut. μνησθήσομαι, *remember*; aor. ἐμνήσθην, *mentioned*

Μίν-ως ὁ, -ω, *Minos*

μισθ-ός ὁ, -οῦ, *payment; reward*

μισθόω, v.t. *let out*; mid. *hire*

μνᾶ ἡ, μνᾶς, *mina, a sum of money amounting to about £4*

μόγις, adv. *with difficulty, reluctantly*

μοῖρ-α ἡ, -ας, *portion, fate; providence*

μόνος, -η, -ον, adj. *alone, only*

μόσχ-ος ὁ, -ου, *calf*

Μουσαῖ-ος ὁ, -ου, *Musaeus*

μοχθηρί-α ἡ, -ας, *wickedness*

μοχθηρ-ός, -ά, -όν, adj. *wretched; bad*

μύρι-ος, -α, -ον, adj. *countless, infinite*; in plur. *ten thousand*

μύ-ωψ ὁ, ἡ, -ωπος, *gadfly*

ναυ-μαχί-α ἡ, -ας, *naval battle*

ναῦς ἡ, νεώς, Homeric dat. plur. νηυσί, *ship*

νέ-ος, -α, -ον, adj. *new, young*

νεότ-ης ἡ, -ητος, *youth; recklessness*

νή, particle, *by* (in oaths, affirmative)

νικάω, v.i. *be victorious*

Νικόστρατ-ος ὁ, -ου, *Nicostratus*

νόθ-ος, -η, -ον, adj. *base-born*

νομίζω, v.t., fut. νομιῶ, aor. ἐνόμισα, *think*; (of gods) *believe in*

νόμ-ος ὁ, -ου, *law*; *custom*

νουθετέω v.t. *admonish*

νοῦς ὁ, νοῦ, *mind, reason*

νυμφ-ή ἡ, -ῆς, *nymph*

νῦν and νυνί, adv. *now*; νῦν δέ, *but as it is*

νύξ ἡ, νυκτός, *night*

νυστάζω, v.i. *doze, be drowsy*

νωθ-ής, -ές, adj. *sluggish*

ξένος, -η, -ον, adj. *strange, foreign*; as noun, *a stranger*

ξένως, adv. of ξένος, *strange to, ignorant of* (with gen.)

ξυγ-γίγνομαι, v.d. *associate with*

ξυγ-γιγνώσκω, v.i. (with dat.), *pardon*

ξυγ-χωρέω, v.t. and i. *concede, yield*; *agree with*

ξυμ-βαίνω, v.i. (for parts see ἀναβαίνω), *agree with, happen*

ξυμ-βάλλω, v.t. (for parts see διαβάλλω), *make up, contribute to*

ξυμ-βουλεύω, v.t. *advise* (with acc. of thing, dat. of pers.)

ξύμ-πας, -πασα, -παν, adj. *all put together*

ξυμ-φεύγω, v.i. *flee with, go into exile with*

ξύν-ειμι, v.i. *be with, associate with*

ξυν-επι-σκοπέω, v.t., fut. -σκέψομαι, *join in considering*

ξυν-ήδη, plup. of ξύνοιδα

ξύν-οιδα, pf., with pres. meaning, *am conscious* (with dat.)

ξυν-ουσί-α ἡ, -ας, *intercourse, society* (so also in plur.)

ξυν-τεταγμένως, adv. *in set terms*

ξυν-τίθημι, v.t. *put together*

ξυν-ωμοσί-α ἡ, -ας, *political club*

ξυν-ωρ-ίς ἡ, -ίδος, *pair of horses*

ὁ, ,ἡ, τό article, *the*; ὁ δέ, *but he*. οἱ μὲν—οἱ δέ, *some —others*

ὅ-δε, ἥδε, τόδε, pron. *this, this here*; dat. fem. as adv. τῇδε, *in this way*

ὀδύρομαι, v.d.t. and i. *weep, bewail*

Ὀδυσσ-εύς ὁ, -έως, *Odysseus*

ὅθεν, conj. *whence*

οἷ, conj. *whither*

οἶδα, pf. with pres. meaning, inf. εἰδέναι, plup. ᾔδη, fut. εἴσομαι, *know*

οἴκαδε, adv. *homewards, home*

οἰκεῖ-ος, -α, -ον, adj. *one's own, personal*; *private*; as noun, *kinsman*

οἰκέω, v.i. *dwell*

οἰκόθεν, adv. *from home*

οἰκο-νομί-α ἡ, -ας, *housekeeping, household economy*

οἶκτ-ος ὁ, -ου, *lamentation*

οἴομαι, v.d.t. and i., fut. οἰήσομαι, *suppose, think, imagine*

οἶ-ος, -α, -ον, adj. *what kind of*; *such as*; οἷός τε, *able*; οἷόν τε, *possible*

οἷός-περ, οἵαπερ, οἷόνπερ, adj. *just such as*

οἶσθα, 2 pres. sing. of οἶδα

οἴχομαι, v.d.i., fut. οἰχή-σομαι, *go away, be gone*

ὀλιγαρχί-α ἡ, -ας, *rule of the few*; *oligarchy*

ὀλίγ-ος, -η, -ον, adj. *small, little*; ὀλίγου, adv. *almost*

ὀλιγωρέω, v.i. *think lightly of, despise*

ὅλ-ος, -η,-ον, adj. *whole*

Ὀλυμπί-ας ἡ, -αδος, *Olympic games* (also in plur.)

Ὅμηρ-ος ὁ, -ου, *Homer*

ὄμνυμι, v.i., fut. ὀμοῦμαι, aor. ὤμοσα, pf. ὀμώμοκα, *swear*

ὁμοίως, adv. *similarly*; *equally*

ὁμο-λογέω, v.i. *agree, confess*

ὅμως, adv. *however, nevertheless*

ὄναρ τό (no gen.), *dream*; as adv. *in a dream*

ὀνειδίζω, v.t., fut. ὀνειδιῶ, *reproach* (with acc. of thing, dat. of pers.)

ὀνίνημι, v.t., fut. ὀνήσω, aor. ὤνησα, *benefit, oblige*; mid. *derive advantage*

ὄνομα τό, -τος, *name, word, phrase*

ὄν-ος ὁ, ἡ, -ου, *donkey*

ὀξ-ύς, -εῖα, -ύ, *sharp, quick*

ὄπη, conj. *in what way*

ὁπηοῦν, adv. *in any way whatever*

ὅπλ-ον τό, -ου, *implement*; pl. *arms*

ὁπόθεν, conj. *whence*

ὅποι, conj. *whither*

ὁπότε, conj. *whenever*

ὁπότερ-ος, -α, -ον, adj. *which of the two?*

ὅπως, (1) adv. *as*; *how* (2) conj. *that, in order that*

ὁπωσ-τι-οῦν, adv. *in any way whatever*

ὁράω, v.t., impf. ἑώρων, fut. ὄψομαι, pf. ἑώρακα, *see*

ὀργ-ή ἡ, -ῆς, *anger*

ὀργίζω, v.t. *provoke*; mid. fut. ὀργιοῦμαι, aor. ὠργίσθην, *be angry*

ὀρθ-ός, -ή, -όν, adj. *right*; adv. ὀρθῶς

ὁρμάω, v.t. and i. *urge on*; *hasten after*; *be eager for*

Ὀρφ-εύς ὁ, -έως, *Orpheus*

ὀρχήστρ-α ἡ, -ας, *Orchestra* (1) *the dancing place in the theatre* (2) *a round terrace near or in the market at Athens.* See note on 26 E

ὅς, ἥ, ὅ, (1) rel. pron. *who, which*; adverbial uses, gen. οὗ, *where*; dat. fem. ᾗ, *in what way* (2) old demonstr. pron. *he*, in the phrase ἦ δ᾽ ὅς, *said he*

ὅσ-ος, -η, -ον, adj. *how great, as great as*; plur. *how many, as many as*

ὅσ-περ, ἥπερ, ὅπερ, pron. *who, which*

119

ὅσ-τις, ἥτις, ὅ τι, contracted gen. ὅτου, dat. ὅτῳ, who, whosoever; he who, inasmuch as he

ὁσ-τισ-οῦν, ὁτιοῦν, pron. any one whatever

ὅταν, conj. whenever

ὅτε, conj. when

ὅτι, conj. that; because

οὐ (οὐκ, οὐχ), neg. particle, not

οὐδαμοῦ, adv. nowhere

οὐδέ, neg. conj. nor; nor yet; not even

οὐδ-είς, οὐδεμία, οὐδέν, numerical adj. no one, none

οὐδε-πώ-ποτε, adv. never at any time

οὐδ-έτερ-ος, -α, -ον, adj. neither of the two

οὐκ-έτι, adv. no longer

οὐκ-οῦν, particle (in questions), so then?

οὖν, particle, therefore, accordingly; then; δ' οὖν, at all events

οὐράνι-ος, -α, -ον, adj. heavenly

οὖς, τό, ὠτός, ear

οὗτος (οὑτοσί), αὕτη, τοῦτο, pron. and adj. this; dat. fem. ταύτῃ, adv. in this way

οὕτω(ς), οὑτωσί, adv. thus, so

ὄφελος τό, in nom. only, worth, benefit, use

ὀφλισκάνω, v.i., fut. ὀφλήσω, aor. ὦφλον (partic. ὄφλων, pf. ὤφληκα, owe, be fined; lose (a lawsuit); with acc. be condemned for

παγ-κάλως, adv. very rightly

πάθ-ος τό, -ους, suffering; experience

παιδεύω, v.t. educate

παιδί-ον τό, -ον, little child

παίζω, v.i. play; joke

παῖς ὁ, παιδός, boy, child

πάλαι, adv. of old, long ago

παλαι-ός, -ά, -όν, adj. old, ancient

Παλαμήδ-ης ὁ, -ους, Palamedes

πάλιν, adv. again, on the other hand

παντάπασι, adv. wholly; by all means

πανταχοῦ, adv. everywhere

πάντως, adv. in any case

πάνυ, adv. altogether, quite, very; (in answers) yes, certainly

παρά, prep.
 (1) with acc. to the side of, to; alongside of; by; contrary to; compared with
 (2) with gen. from the side of, from
 (3) with dat. at the side of, near, with

παρά-δειγμα τό, -τος, example

παρ-αιτέομαι, v.d.t. beg of, entreat

παρα-κέλευσ-ις ἡ, -εως, exhortation

παρα-κελεύω, v.i. exhort (with dat.)

παρα-λαμβάνω, v.t. take charge of, take possession of

Πάραλ-ος, ὁ, -ον, Paralus

παρα-μένω, v.i. remain with (with dat.)

παρά-νομ-ος, -ον, adj. contrary to law; adv. παρα-νόμως

παρά-παν, adv. altogether, entirely

παρα-πλησίως, adv. much the same as

παρα-σκευάζω, v.t. prepare

παρα-χωρέω, v.i. make way, stand aside

πάρ-ειμι, v.i. be present; in partic. ὁ παρών, the bystander

παρ-έχω, v.t. provide, offer (so also in mid.)

παρ-ίημι, v.t. omit; mid. παρ-ίεμαι entreat

Πάριος, adj. Parian

πᾶς, πᾶσα, πᾶν, adj. all, every

πάσχω, v.t., fut. πείσομαι, aor. ἔπαθον, pf. πέπονθα, experience, suffer; be treated

πατ-ήρ ὁ, -ρός, father

Πάτροκλ-ος ὁ, -ου, Patroclus

παύω, v.t. check, stop; mid. cease

πείθω, v.t., fut., πείσω, aor. ἔπεισα, pf. πέπεικα, persuade; str. pf. πέποιθα and mid. (with dat.) obey; trust; listen to; verbal neut. adj. πειστέον, one must persuade; one must obey

πειράομαι, v.d.t., fut. πειράσομαι, try, attempt

πέμπτ-ος, -η, -ον, adj. fifth

πέν-ης ὁ, -ητος, poor man

πενί-α ἡ, -ας, poverty

πέντε, numerical adj. indecl. five

περ, particle, emphasises the word to which it is annexed, indeed, even

περί, prep. with acc., gen., and dat., around, about, concerning

περὶ πολλοῦ (πλείστου) ποιεῖσθαι, to set a high (the highest) value on

περι-άπτω, v.t. fasten around; bring upon

περι-γίγνομαι, v.d.i. get the better of, be superior to (with gen.)

περί-ειμι, v.i. go about

περι-εργάζομαι, v.d.i., do too much; be a busybody

περι-έρχομαι, v.d.i., go about

περι-μένω, v.t. and i. wait

περισσ-ός, -ή, -όν, adj. out of the way; excessive

περι-φέρω, v.t. carry about; swing about

πέτρ-α ἡ, -ας (Homeric -η, -ης), stone

πιθανῶς, adv. persuasively

πιστεύω, v.t. and i. believe (with dat.), trust

πλάν-η ἡ, ης, wandering

πλάττω, v.t., fut. πλάσω, aor. ἔπλασα, fashion, make up

Πλάτ-ων ὁ, -ωνος, Plato

πλέ-ων or πλεί-ων, -ον, comp. of πολύς, more; πλέον ποιεῖν, be successful; superl. πλεῖστος

πλῆθ-ος τό, -ους, multitude; mob; democratic party

πλημμέλει-α ἡ, -ας, false note (in music); mistake

πλήν, conj. and prep. with gen. except

πλησίον, adv. and prep. with gen. *near*

πλούσι-ος, -α, -ον, adj. *rich*

ποδαπ-ός -ή, -όν, adj. *from what country?*

πόθεν, adv. *whence*

ποιέω, v.t. *make, do, write poetry*; mid. ποιοῦμαι, *make for oneself; count, consider, deem*

ποίημα τό, -τος, *poem*

ποίησ-ις ή, -εως, *poetry*

ποιητ-ής ὁ, -οῦ, *poet*

πόλεμ-ος ὁ, -ον, *war*

πόλ-ις ή, -εως, *city*

πολίτ-ης, ὁ, -ον, *citizen*

πολιτικ-ός, -ή, -όν, adj. *belonging to a citizen, civic*

πολλάκις, adv. *often*

πολλαχοῦ, adv. *in many places*

πολύς, πολλή, πολύ, *much, great, vehement*; plur. *many*; οἱ πολλοί, *the majority*; τὸ πολύ, *the greater part*

πονέω, v.i. *labour, toil*

πονηρί-α ή, -ας, *wickedness, depravity*

πονηρ-ός, -ά, -όν, adj. *depraved, bad*

πόν-ος ὁ, -ον, *labour*

πόρρω, adv. and prep. with gen. *far; far advanced in*

πόσ-ος, -η, -ον, adj. *how great; how many*

πότε, adv. *when?*

ποτε, particle, *at some time, ever*; τίς ποτε, *who in the world?*

Ποτείδαι-α ή, -ας, *Potidaea*

πότερον, πότερα, adv. *whether*

πότμ-ος ὁ, -ον, *doom*

που, adv. *somewhere; anywhere; I suppose*

πρᾶγμα τό, -τος, *act; thing; business*; plur. sometimes *trouble*

πραγματεύομαι, v.d.t. and i. *exert oneself; be engaged in*; pass. *be elaborated*

πρᾶξ-ις ή, -εως, *action, business, matter*

πράττω, v.t. and i., fut. πράξω, aor. ἔπραξα, pf. πέπραχα, *do, make*; with adverbs (εὖ, κακῶς) (*well, badly*), *fare*, str. pf. πέπραγα; mid. *exact* (money) *for oneself*

πρέπω, v.i. *suit*; πρέπει, impers. *it becomes, it is fitting* (with dat.)

πρεσβ-ύς, -εῖα, -ύ, adj. *old; elder*

πρίαμαι, v.d. *buy*

πρίν, adv. and conj. *before, until*

πρό, prep. with gen. *before; in comparison with; sooner than*

Πρόδικ-ος ὁ, -ον, *Prodicus*

προ-θυμέομαι, v.d.t. *be eager, be zealous*

προῖκα, adv. *for nothing, gratis*

προ-κρίνω, v.t. *prefer before, set over*

πρός, prep.
  (1) with acc. *to, towards; against; with a view to*
  (2) with gen. *from; at the hands of; by* (in entreaties)
  (3) with dat. *close to; in addition to*

προσ-δοκάω, v.t. and i. *expect*

πρόσ-ειμι, v.i. *go up to, approach* (with dat.)

προσ-έρχομαι, v.d.i. *meet, come across* (with dat.)

προσ-έχω, v.t. *apply*

προσ-ήκ-ων, -ον, adj. (partic. of προσήκω), *proper, befitting; related*; as noun, *relative*

πρόσθεν, adv. *before*

προσ-καθίζω, v.i. *sit down by; settle on*

πρόσ-κειμαι, v.d.i. *settle upon; attack* (with dat.)

πρόσ-οιδα, pf. with pres. meaning, *owe in addition*

προσ-ποιέομαι, v.d.t. *pretend*

προσ-τάττω, v.t. *give orders to*

προσ-τίθημι, v.t. *apply; bestow*

προσ-χράομαι, v.d.i. *make use of for* (with dat.)

πρότερ-ος, -α, -ον, comp. adj. *former*; adv. **πρότερον**, *before*

προ-τρέπω, v.t. *urge forward*

πρόχειρ-ος, -ον, adj. *ready to hand; easy; obvious*

πρυτανεῖ-ον τό, -ον, *Prytaneum*

πρυτανεύω, v.i. *be in office on the Council at Athens*

Πρύταν-ις ὁ, -εως, *Prytanis*

πρῶτ-ος, -η, -ον, superl. adj. *first*; adv. **πρῶτον**, *first*

Πυθί-α ἡ, -ας, *the priestess of Apollo at Delphi*

πυκν-ός, -ή, -όν, adj. *close-set; frequent*

πῶλ-ος ὁ, -ον, *foal*

πώ-ποτε, adv. *ever yet*

πῶς, adv. *how?* πως, *haply, somehow*

Ῥαδάμανθ-υς ὁ, -νος, *Rhadamanthys*

ῥᾴδι-ος, -α, -ον, adj. *easy*; comp. ῥᾴων, superl. ῥᾷστος. ῥᾳδίως, adv. *easily, lightly*

ῥῆμα τό, -τος, *word*

ῥητέον, verbal neut. adj. (from ἐρῶ), *it must be said*

ῥήτ-ωρ ὁ, -ορος, *orator*

Σαλαμίνι-ος, -α, -ον, adj. *belonging to Salamis*

Σαλαμ-ίς ἡ, -ῖνος, *Salamis*

σαυτ-όν, -οῦ, pron. (no nom.), *thyself*

σαφῶς, adv. *clearly*; comp. σαφέστερον; superl. σαφέστατα

σελήν-η ἡ, -ης, *moon*

σημεῖ-ον τό, -ον, *sign*

σιγάω, v.i. *be silent*

Σίσυφ-ος ὁ, -ον, *Sisyphus*

σιτέομαι, v.d. *feed; maintain*

σίτησ-ις ἡ, -εως, *maintenance*

σκέπτομαι, v.d.t., fut. σκέψομαι, aor. ἐσκεψάμην, pf. ἔσκεμμαι, *consider, examine*

σκια-μαχέω, v.i. *fight against shadows*

σκοπέω, v.t. *consider, examine*, in pres. and impf.; other tenses as if from **σκέπτομαι**

σμικρός is the same as μικρός

σός, σή, σόν, poss. adj. *thy*

σοφί-α ἡ, -ας, *wisdom*

σοφιστ-ής ὁ, -οῦ, *sophist*

σοφ-ός, -ή, -όν, adj. *wise, clever*

σπουδάζω, v.i. *be serious; have zeal for*

σπουδ-ή ἡ, -ῆς, *haste, earnestness;* dat. used adverbially, *in earnest*

στάσ-ις ἡ, -εως, *faction*

στρατηγί-α ἡ, -ας, *military command*

στρατηγ-ός ὁ, -οῦ, *general*

στρατι-ά ἡ, -ᾶς, *army, expedition*

σύ, pron. σοῦ or σου, *thou*

σφεῖς, pron. σφῶν, *themselves*

Σφήττι-ος, -α, -ον, adj. *belonging to the deme Sphettus*

σφόδρα, adv. *emphatically*

σφοδρ-ός, -α, -ον, adj. *vehement;* adv. σφοδρῶς

σχεδόν, adv. *nearly*

σχολ-ή ἡ, -ῆς, *leisure*

σώζω, v.t. *save*

Σωκράτ-ης ὁ, -ους, *Socrates*

σῶμα τό, -τος, *body*

τάν in ὦ τάν, *good sir*

τάξ-ις ἡ, -εως, *arrangement, post*

τάττω, v.t., fut. τάξω, *arrange; station; draw up*

ταυτί is the same as ταῦτα; -ί indicates a gesture

τάχα, adv. *may be, probably*

τάχ-ος τό, -ους, *speed;* διὰ ταχέων, *speedily*

ταχ-ύς, -εῖα, -ύ, adj. *swift;* comp. θάττων, superl. τάχιστος

τε, conj. *both, and*

τεκμήρι-ον τό, -ου, *sign*

Τελάμ-ων ὁ, -ῶνος, *Telamon*

τελευτάω, v.i. *come to an end; die;* partic. τελευτῶν, *at last, in the end*

τελέω, v.t., fut. τελέσω or τελῶ, aor. ἐτέλεσα, pf. τετέλεκα, *complete; fulfil; pay*

τέτταρ-ες, -α, numerical adj. *four*

τέχν-η ἡ, -ης, *art, craft, trade*

τηλικ-όσ-δε, -ήδε, -όνδε, and τηλικ-οῦτος, -αύτη, -οῦτον, adj. *of such an age*

τίθημι, v.t., fut. θήσω, aor. ἔθηκα, pf. τέθεικα, *place; set down*

τιμάω, v.t. *honour;* mid. *propose a penalty*

τιμ-ή ἡ, -ῆς, *honour; penalty*

τίμημα τό, -τος, *penalty, award*

τιμωρέω, v.t. *avenge* (with acc. of the crime and dat. of the pers.); mid. *avenge oneself on, take revenge on* (with acc. of the pers.)

τιμωρί-α ἡ, -ας, *punishment, revenge*

τις, τι, pron., gen. τινος or του, dat. τινι or τῳ, nom. plur. n. τινα or ἄττα, *some one, some; a certain;* τι, as adv. *in some way, somewhat*

τίς, τί, pron. *who? what?* as adv. τί, *why?*

τοι, particle, *in truth, verily*;
καί τοι, *and yet, however*

τοι-όσ-δε, -άδε, -όνδε, adj.
and τοι-οῦτος, -αύτη,
-οῦτο(ν), adj. *such*

τολμάω, v.t. *dare, venture*

τολμ-ή ή, -ῆς, *daring, audacity*

τόπ-ος ό, -ου, *place*

τοσ-όσ-δε, -ήδε, -όνδε, adj.
so many

τοσ-οῦτος, -αύτη, -οῦτο(ν),
adj. *so great, so much*; plur.
so many

τότε, adv. *then*

τοὐναντίον, contracted for
τὸ ἐναντίον

τραγῳδί-α ή, -ας, *tragedy*

τράπεζ-α ή, -ης, *banker's
table*

τρεῖς, τρία, numerical adj.
three

τρέπω, v.t., fut. τρέψω, aor.
ἔτρεψα, aor. mid. ἐτρα-
πόμην, pf. pass. τέτραμμαι,
turn; mid. *turn oneself*; *betake
oneself to*

τρέφω, v.t., fut. θρέψω, pf.
τέτροφα, pf. pass. τέθραμ-
μαι, *nourish, bring up*

τριάκοντα, numerical adj.
indecl. *thirty*

Τριπτόλεμ-ος ό, -ου, *Triptolemus*

Τροί-α ή, -ας, *Troy*

τρόπ-ος ό, -ου, *way, manner,
fashion*

τροφ-ή ή, -ῆς, *nourishment;
support*

τυγχάνω, v.i., fut. τεύξομαι,
aor. ἔτυχον, pf. τετύχηκα,
meet with, happen; τυγχάνω
ὤν, *happen to be*

ὕβρ-ις ή, -εως, *insolence*

ὑβριστ-ής ό, -οῦ, *insolent man*

υἱ-ός ό, -οῦ, plur. υἱεῖς, *son*

ὑμ-εῖς, -ῶν, pron. *you, ye*

ὑμέτερ-ος, -α, -ον, poss. adj.
your

ὑπ-είκω, v.i., fut. -είξω, aor.
-εῖξα, or -είκαθον, *yield,
give way to*

ὑπέρ, prep.
(1) with acc., *beyond, over*
(2) with gen., *above, over,
about, on behalf of*

ὑπ-έχω, v.t. *undergo, suffer*

ὑπηρεσί-α ή, -ας, *service*

ὑπισχνέομαι, v.d.t. (en-
larged from ὑπέχομαι), fut.
ὑποσχήσομαι, aor. ὑπ-
εσχόμην, pf. ὑπέσχημαι,
promise

ὕπν-ος ό, -ου, *sleep*

ὑπό, prep. with acc. *under*
(motion to); with gen. *by*
(agent); *owing to*; *under*
(rest under); with dat.
under (rest under)

ὑπο-λαμβάνω, v.i. *take up;
interrupt, reply; suppose*

ὑπο-λογίζομαι, v.d.t. *reckon
in, take account of*

ὑπο-μένω, v.t. and i. *endure;
submit to*

ὑπο-στέλλω, v.t. fut. -στελῶ,
aor. ὑπέστειλα, pf. ὑπ-
έσταλκα, *contract*; mid. *dis-
semble, suppress*

ὕστερ-ος, -α, -ον, adj.
following, later

φαίνω, v.t. and i., fut. φανῶ,
aor. ἔφηνα, pf. (i.) πέφηνα,
show, shine; in mid. and
pass. **φαίνομαι**, *be shown,
appear*

φάσκω, v.t. *allege, assert*

φαῦλ-ος, -η, -ον, adj. *worth-
less, paltry, common*

φείδομαι, v.d.i., fut. φείσο-
μαι, *spare* (with gen.)

φέρω, v.t., fut. οἴσω, aor.
ἤνεγκον, pf. ἐνήνοχα, *bear,
bring*; (in exhortations)
φέρε, *come*

φεύγω, v.t. and i., fut. φεύξομαι and φευξοῦμαι, aor.
ἔφυγον, pf. πέφευγα, *flee,
escape*; *be defendant* (in a
lawsuit)

φήμ-η ἡ, -ης, *rumour*

φημί, v.t. and i., 2 pers. sing.
impf. ἔφησθα, *say, speak*

φθονέω, v.i. *envy, grudge*

φθόν-ος ὁ, -ου, *envy, jealousy*

φιλέω, v.t. *love*

φιλό-πολις, gen. φιλοπό-
λιδος, adj. *loving one's city,
patriotic*

φίλ-ος, -η, -ον, adj. *dear*; as
noun, *a friend*

φιλο-σοφέω, v.i. *study philosophy*

φιλό-τιμ-ος, -ον, adj. *loving
honour*; *ambitious*

φιλο-ψυχί-α ἡ, -ας, *love of
life*

φλυαρέω, v.i. (with cognate
acc.) *talk nonsense*

φλυαρί-α ἡ, -ας, *nonsense*

φοβέω, v.t. *frighten*; mid.
and pass. *fear, be afraid*

φορτικ-ός, -ή, -όν, adj.
wearisome; *vulgar*

φράζω, v.t. *point out, show, tell*

φρόνησ-ις ἡ, -εως, *prudence,
wisdom*

φρόνιμ-ος, -ον, adj. *reasonable*, adv. **φρονίμως**;
φρονίμως ἔχειν, *to be
wise, sensible*

φροντίζω, v.i., fut. φροντιῶ,
aor. ἐφρόντισα, pf. πεφρόν-
τικα, *think about, heed*; *care
for* (with gen.)

φροντιστ-ής ὁ, -οῦ, *thinker,
speculator, contemplator*

φυγ-ή ἡ, -ῆς, *flight*; *banishment*

φύσ-ις ἡ, -εως, *nature*

φύω, v.t. and i., fut. φύσω,
wk. aor. ἔφυσα, *make to
grow*, mid., with str. aor.
ἔφυν, pf. πέφυκα, *grow, spring
from*

φων-ή ἡ, -ῆς, *voice, language*

Χαιρεφ-ῶν ὁ, -ῶντος,
Chaerephon

χαίρω, v.i., fut. χαιρήσω, str.
aor. pass. with act. meaning ἐχάρην, pf. κεχάρηκα,
rejoice

χαλεπαίνω, v.i., fut. χαλε-
πανῶ, aor. ἐχαλέπηνα, *be
angry with* (with dat.)

χαλεπ-ός, -ή, -όν, adj. *difficult, troublesome*

χαριεντίζομαι, v.d., fut.
χαριεντιοῦμαι, *jest*

χαρίζομαι, v.d.t. and i., fut.
χαριοῦμαι, aor. ἐχαρισάμην,
pf. κεχάρισμαι, *gratify, show
favour to* (with dat.)

126